MW00613142

WETHERSFIELD INSTITUTE
Proceedings, 1993

# CHRISTIANITY AND WESTERN CIVILIZATION

# Christianity and Western Civilization

## Christopher Dawson's Insight:

### Can a Culture Survive the Loss of Its Religious Roots?

Papers Presented at a Conference
Sponsored by the Wethersfield Institute
*New York City, October 15, 1993*

IGNATIUS PRESS    SAN FRANCISCO

Cover photo courtesy of
*The Chesterton Review*
Saskatoon, Saskatchewan
Cover design by Riz Boncan Marsella

Published 1995, Ignatius Press, San Francisco
© 1993 Homeland Foundation
ISBN 0-89870-534-7
Library of Congress catalogue number 94-79296
Printed in the United States of America

## Wethersfield Institute
## Statement of Purpose

The purpose of the Wethersfield Institute is to promote a clear understanding of Catholic teaching and practice and to explore the cultural and intellectual dimensions of the Catholic Faith. The Institute does so in practical ways that include seminars, colloquies and conferences, especially as they pursue our goals on a scientific and scholarly level. The Institute publishes its proceedings.

It is also interested in projects that advance those subjects. The Institute usually sponsors them directly, but also joins with accredited agencies that share our interests.

Msgr. Eugene V. Clark, President
E. Lisk Wyckoff, Jr., Vice President
Patricia P. Donahoe, Program Director

# CONTENTS

# CONTRIBUTORS

JAMES HITCHCOCK is Professor of History at St. Louis University, St. Louis, Missouri.

RUSSELL HITTINGER is Professor of Philosophy at Catholic University, Washington, D.C.

JOSEPH KOTERSKI, S.J., is Professor of Philosophy at Fordham University, Bronx, New York.

GLENN W. OLSEN is Professor of History at the University of Utah in Salt Lake City, Utah.

ROBERT V. YOUNG is Professor of English at North Carolina State University in Raleigh.

CARL SCHMITT

# PREFACE

"Can a culture survive the loss of its religious roots?"

In 1993, when the Wethersfield Institute prepared for its fall conference, "Christianity and Western Civilization", the name of Christopher Dawson inevitably came to the fore—indeed it seemed that it should be prominent in the conference.

The reader, therefore, may find it curious that none of the papers deals directly with Dawson himself or with his achievements. Yet none of the papers escapes his strong influence: Christopher Dawson stands as an inspiration and guiding presence behind them all.

The volume is a testimony to the stature of the man. His life was devoted to excellent scholarly work as a sociologist and historian; but his principal achievement and contemporary impact are in his profound insights into the relationship of religion and culture. Dawson is well known for his belief that religion and culture are wedded to one another and that the study of any society must include its religious dimension. But he did more than that: he researched the matter deeply, and his study drew on a learning whose range is astonishing. He wrote both for scholars and for a wide reading public.

At the same time, his personal faith in God, in Christ and his Church led him to study the special dynamism of the Church through its power of renewal. Because he perceived that dynamism, he did not become—as many of his contemporaries did—a mere celebrator of the achievements of the Middle Ages. He was able to assess Christian culture as a continuous tradition, in good times and in bad—and make abundantly clear how a culture deprived of its religious root is moribund. While his two series of Gifford Lectures are perhaps his best known (with *Religion and the Rise of Western Culture* the better known of the two), his treatment of the barbarian world that followed the fall of Rome and of the French Revolution has contributed richly to our understanding of those critical periods.

All of this has made Dawson's thought important in our time. Indeed, he is something of a prophet—in the finest sense of that word. For—to use three expressions drawn from the titles of three of his books—in his mind it was clear that "the judgment of the nations" is ever present; yet his sense of optimism about "Christianity and the new age" rested on the strength of Christianity ever involved in a battle—the battle of "the sword of the Spirit".

The Wethersfield Institute considers itself very much engaged in these questions and found the insights of Christopher Dawson central to its fall conference of 1993. It was inevitable that Christopher Dawson should exert a constant, almost personal presence in the papers presented here. It was appropriate, too, that the Institute, in a reception following the conference on October 15, 1993, should have given a special honor to John J. Mulloy, who, tirelessly, for over four decades has done so much to bring Dawson's thought before the American reading public.

# SALUTATION
# FOR MR. JOHN J. MULLOY

Throughout the day we have been trying to steep ourselves in the thought of Christopher Dawson. But without the tireless efforts of the man we now want to honor, John J. Mulloy of Fayetteville, Arkansas, we would have nowhere near the amount of Dawson material available to us nor would Dawson be so widely known.

Dawson's own learning was the result of patient scholarship carried out privately and quietly, but his natural reticence made him shy of the public stage. We owe it to Mr. Mulloy that he made his American lecture tour and that volumes like *Dynamics of World History* ever appeared. Dawson's books from 1933 onward tend to be collections of articles previously published in diverse journals joined to articles elicited for American magazines by Mr. Mulloy's steady stream of letters to Dawson. In those letters he urged Dawson to develop one or another aspect of his ideas about world history, or the comparison of the oriental world religions with Christianity, or the study of Christian culture in American schools. Without the stimulus Mulloy gave Dawson, many of the insights Dawson has left us might never have been committed to paper.

Among Mr. Mulloy's many other accomplishments, let us simply note two: (1) some 130 articles on "The Catholic Tradition" that appeared between 1973 and 1983 in *The Wanderer*, covering a wide range of historical and topical issues, and (2) the work of the Society for Christian Culture. Since 1981 the SCC has joined other groups in sponsoring ten conferences and has produced ten volumes of *The Dawson Newsletter*, which makes available short articles by Dawson and provides analyses of many subjects related to Christian culture and to Dawson's thought. Mr. Mulloy, our sincere thanks for your labors!

JOSEPH KOTERSKI, S.J.

# RELIGION AS THE ROOT OF CULTURE

Christopher Dawson is best known as an historian and sociologist who focused on the relation of religion to culture.
Though he has many specialized studies of particular events
and trends—the French Revolution, for instance, or the Oxford Movement[1]—he is equally a master of "the big picture",
and it is on his thesis that religion is the root of culture that I
would like to focus here.

"Religion", says Dawson, "is the key of history."[2] In contrast to the academic tendency to reduce religion to an epiphe-
nomenon, a product of various material and psychic forces (the
recipe depending for the most part on how much Marxism and
how much Freudianism one likes to mix in the intoxicated con-
versations at Ivy League faculty clubs), Dawson insists on the
need to understand a society's religion if one wants to understand the original formation and the successive transformations
of any human culture:

> In all ages the first creative works of a culture are due to a reli-
> gious inspiration and dedicated to a religious end. The temples
> of the gods are the most enduring works of man. Religion stands
> at the threshold of all the great literatures of the world. Philo-
> sophy is its offspring and is a child which constantly returns to
> its parent. And the same is true of social institutions. Kingship
> and law are religious institutions and even today they have not
> entirely divested themselves of their numinous character, as we
> can see in the English coronation rite and in the formulas of
> our law courts. All the institutions of family and marriage and
> kinship have a religious background and have been maintained
> and are still maintained by formidable social sanctions.[3]

This general thesis Dawson articulates in the first volume of his 1947–1948 Gifford Lectures, *Religion and Culture*, which is devoted to the comparative study of religion. In the second set of lectures, *Religion and the Rise of Western Culture*, he deals specifically with the religious origins of our own Western culture and the patterns of its growth as "a series of renaissances—of spiritual and intellectual revivals which arose independently, usually under religious influences, and were transmitted by a spontaneous process of free communication"[4] to lands other than the locale where they originated. This is a phenomenon we still see at work today in the universal hunger for Western science-and-technology transfer and in the global hankering after democratic forms of government, even where social preparations for the civil restraint required to make democracy work are not yet sufficiently in place.[5]

But however much the West is admired, openly or with secret jealousy, legitimate concern arises over where we are headed. Will, for instance, the easier access to material goods promised by westernization simply drown thirsty Eastern Europe in hedonism? Or, to consider America and Western Europe, will the relentless secularization even of religious institutions desiccate the very sources of the cultural life of the West?[6] There is no shortage of prophets of doom who think it already has, and the massive evidence available is compelling.

Our culture certainly does not feel like a religious culture. Even the Catholic subculture in which many here in the audience grew up seems to be in shambles. The prevailing wisdom among the most successful, prosperous and lively sectors of our society—the media, the legal and medical professions, the professoriate and the wizards of technology—is that this culture has a fine life of its own and plenty of drive; religion is better left a private matter, available to the superstitious but invariably a bull in a china shop when it enters the arena of public policy discussions. At best, religion is considered an inspiration to the good manners and morals needed in civic life, so there is no harm in paying it lip service, so long as the rhetoric is sufficiently pluralistic and innocuously inclusive.

Bleak as the prospect of restoring the spiritual dimension of our culture any time soon is, there is a more constructive assessment possible than merely gloomy despair. We dare not be naïve about this. The irrepressible optimism of the sixties brought many well-intentioned religious leaders to expect no harm to come from exchanging a predominantly eschatological model of religion (concern with saving one's own soul and one's neighbor's) for the social gospel of liberal Protestantism (the reduction of Christianity to part of its ethical and moral teachings).[7] But the reason for hope even amid the current confusion consists in the increasing recognition that the task of the Church is direct evangelization and that the renewal of culture is its hoped-for fruit.[8] Like any good apple or peach, the fruit may be what we most directly enjoy, but in the long-range perspective of the tree, the moisture and nutriments in the fruit actually help to root the seed in some new ground so it may gradually but sturdily grow, transforming the land and the landscape as it does so.

To appreciate the call to refocus religious energy on direct, one-to-one personal evangelization as a genuine blessing and not a fall-back strategy of desperation requires that we see "the big picture" of the proper relation of religion and culture. In what follows, I would like to develop two points: (1) Dawson's analysis of the distinctive trait specific to the Christian religion as formative of Western culture, and (2) an important shift the Church has been laboring to make in this regard.

## Religion and the Rise of Western Culture

Judaism and Christianity constitute the religious pole in the formation of Western culture coordinate with the legal, scientific and philosophical pole of Greece and Rome. While a pragmatist may hold history to be irrelevant and a committed pluralist might explain it away on the grounds that some religious factor or other is a necessary component in the rise of all the other great world cultures, Dawson's point is that the specific type of religious influence Christianity has exerted is unparalleled, and the effect upon Western culture has been unique. By its balance between transcendence and immanence —worship of an utterly transcendent God, creator of a universe wholly other than himself, and reverence for the world God made and loved so much that the Word became incarnate for its healing and restoration—Christianity has taken a distinctive stance toward the world: it is in the world but not entirely of it; in the phrases of the Gospel, one must render to Caesar what is Caesar's but to God what is God's. Augustine's doctrine of the Two Cities[9] is a Western political formulation of one of Christianity's nonnegotiable principles: genuine interest and love for this world, but always from an unyielding desire to renew the world, whatever degree of cultural progress or regress it finds in a given land at a given time, in order to transform this world in light of a higher love, its religious bond to the triune God. The cultural result is a flexibility and dynamism that accepts and even encourages the development of new social forms that protect and enhance such characteristically Western ideals as freedom and autonomy.

By contrast, other great world religions have tended to idealize a timeless and unchanging perfection within the world and have fashioned their cultures according to some sacred social order, for instance the Confucian state in China or the Indian caste system.[10] This is why social freedom, change and autonomy are deeply threatening "Western values" that have so unsettled these ancient orders, especially when they arrive shorn of the religious orientation in which they were born and in which we find them so fruitful for the spiritual life. How easy it is for us to talk about freedom of worship, faith as a free act of assent, freedom of opportunity to use the goods of this world, popular determination in matters of politics, responsible moral freedom, and the like. But there is no one of us who does not tremble before the perversions to which these notions are put in our own society when proper religious guidance is removed—we need only think of the connotations that such phrases as "freedom of choice" have come to have, or think how often people argue that moral autonomy means that "no one imposes his or her morality on me" without reflecting on the fact that it is only ordered liberty and the social embodiment of certain moral principles in law that guarantee whatever autonomy we exercise.

Islam offers a classic picture of how a religious perspective on life and a set of religious doctrines can entirely change a social way of living. Our closest contact with this influence may be with that portion of the American black community which has become Muslim. But it is important to recall how the social forms and institutions this religion has created have spread across racial and geographical boundaries—from Saudi Arabia and the whole Mideast to the very different situations of nations on the coast of West Africa like Nigeria, the islands of Malaysia, large portions of India and poor war-torn Bosnia. Once Islam achieves dominance in a region, its social forms become set and remain fixed for centuries, with as simple and clear a design as its single line of creed, Allah alone is God, and Muhammed is his prophet.[11]

By contrast, Western culture is known for its dynamism and constant readiness to change (what Dawson called its "series of renaissances" has become parodied in the American tendency to reinvent ourselves every ten minutes), and yet Western culture only succeeded in avoiding anarchy while championing such broad notions of freedom by retaining both poles, an orientation to the transcendent as well as a concern for the cultivation and manipulation of the material world. There is a cosmic struggle between forces of good and evil for the soul of mankind that is being fought here. Material progress needs to be kept in the service of spiritual freedom and not become, as it often does today, an end in itself. In the following passage from *The Judgement of the Nations*, Dawson links this development of political freedom to spiritual insights about moral responsibility:

> Christian freedom combined and transformed the elements of barbaric freedom and classical citizenship into something new. . . . This sense of Christian liberty . . . was diffused throughout the whole body of Christendom and formed the spiritual background which from an external point of view often appears extremely hierarchic and authoritarian. In Eastern Europe, owing largely to the Oriental imperialisms, to which it was so long subjected, this background was so far removed from political realities that the Christian social consciousness expressed itself in mystical or apocalyptic terms. In the West, however, the social order was more plastic and more organically related to the beliefs and ideals of the people. In fact, no civilization, not even that of ancient Greece, has ever undergone such a continuous and profound process of change as Western Europe has done during the last 900 years. It is impossible to explain this fact in purely economic terms by a materialistic interpretation of history. The principle of change has been a spiritual one and the progress of Western civilization is intimately related to the dynamic ethos of Western Christianity, which has gradually made Western man conscious of his moral responsibility and his duty to change the world.[12]

Yet in the material success of the West, its sources have been forgotten, or even disparaged. The godlessness of the Humanist Movement today, for instance, belies the religious roots of Humanism in the Renaissance. Although the fifteenth century version was genuinely a movement of return to nature, especially after the emptiness of philosophical nominalism and the terrifying voluntarism that had been let loose in politics, the vision of the human being which Humanists like Francis Bacon and Thomas More rediscovered was not simply that of the state of nature but that fashioned by a millennium of Christianity:

> the human type that had been produced by ten centuries of spiritual discipline and intensive cultivation of the inner life. The

great men of the Renaissance were spiritual men even when they were most deeply immersed in the temporal order. It was from the accumulated resources of their Christian past that they acquired the energy to conquer the material world and to create the new spiritual culture.[13]

Even in the darker periods of the eighteenth century Enlightenment and nineteenth century imperialism, when the West set out to conquer the world and, for better or worse, to transform it into its own image, it is possible to see, even in its distortion, a distinctive mark this religion brought to bear: the urge to expand one's intellectual horizons and to spread one's own culture. The cynics who so ravaged Columbus during the 1992 quincentenary might be quick to acknowledge this distinctive mark, "Yes, a ruthless quest for domination." But Dawson offers a judicious reminder:

It is easy enough to present the history of this European expansion as a process of imperialistic aggression and economic exploitation. But aggression and exploitation are nothing new in world history, and if they suffice to explain the European achievement, it might have been realized hundreds or thousands of years earlier by any of the world empires that have successively held the stage of history. The peculiar achievement of Western culture in modern times is due to a new element which was not present in the older type of imperialism.[14]

What is this new element present alongside the admitted lust for power and wealth so prominent in European history like every other history? Dawson calls it Western culture's "missionary character":

Even in the darkest periods of the Middle Ages this dynamic principle continued to operate. For what distinguishes Western culture from the other world civilizations is its *missionary character* —its transmission from one people to another in a continuous series of spiritual movements.[15]

The bulk of Dawson's second set of Gifford Lectures is then dedicated to showing how such distinctively Western social institutions as the medieval commune and guild, school and university emerged from this missionary thrust.

The original movement from east to west with the generations of missionaries that sprang from St. Paul and St. Irenaeus laid the foundations of Western Christianity. When the Empire fell, Christians of what had been the western provinces of Rome carried the process of transmission to the barbarian peoples of the North: St. Patrick to Ireland and the agents of St. Gregory the Great to England. In the sixth century the direction was reversed, and missionaries of such newly Christian lands as Ireland and England set about the evangelization of Dutch and German pagans and the reform of the Frankish Church, with the attendant cultural fruit of a revival of education and classical learning.[16] Unlike Byzantium, where political power and cultural hegemony coincided, Western culture from this period manifests a dualism that has constantly supported the development of freedom and the dynamic growth of new forms of social organization. The spread of monasteries, for instance, can be traced to a quest for individual perfection and salvation, but without doubt it also made for the renewal of urban culture in the Middle Ages and eventually for the directly responsive civil government frequently found in the High Middle Ages. Likewise, monastic reform spread from place to place in the tenth and eleventh centuries and spurred the reform of the Church in general. The rise of the universities as centers for research and the dissemination of learning was enabled by the relative ease of communication and participation among those of diverse national origin; to this day, even though most university education is thoroughly secular, the ideal of what a university is continues to bear the marks of seeking the advancement of knowledge and the spread of learning with which this religious culture originally endowed the institution. The participants shared a common culture, but one tolerant of regional diversity and all the more colorful and interesting thereby. This same vitality is evident in the massive cultural effect of the new mendicant orders in the twelfth and thirteenth centuries. The preaching of the Dominicans reinvigorated religiously tepid towns, and the witness to poverty in the very life of the Franciscans made their preaching of the Gospel as credible as it was enchanting.

The period of missionary effort that more easily springs to the mind is the grand effort that followed the discovery of the Americas and the opening of sea routes to the East. Current critics of the genuine abuses all too often practiced upon the peoples native to the lands claimed and conquered by Europeans speedily tar the religious impulse of the missionaries with the same brush, forgetful of the selfless service these missionaries were offering to peoples who had never heard of Christ. If the history of this period is checkered, it is only right to acknowledge the light squares running in the same direction as the dark. In fact, it was precisely reflection on the spiritual liberation from ignorance and sin being promoted by these missionaries that brought intellectuals of the universities to reconsider the moral question of slavery (a practice which students are regularly shocked to learn that an enlightened Greek like Aristotle had no qualms in justifying) and begin the process of its condemnation that took centuries to complete.

Our concern with grasping "the big picture" permits us to forego a rehearsal of further details. Dawson shows us a picture of Western culture dynamic in its social forms as the result of a religion whose mission is to carry the Good News to the ends of the earth. As its believers found their understanding of where those ends of the earth were, so their missionary efforts were directed. At the same time, the vision of human dignity as made in the image and likeness of God continued to develop and required the constant development of social forms worthy of such a being: schools and universities for the training of the mind, for example, or civil and economic organizations that protected the common good and personal labor. The constant danger of such fluidity was the opportunity of interested parties to strive for absolutist solutions, whether from the imperial or papal parties, especially, as Dawson points out, once the centers of reform concentrated in northern Europe were alienated from the principle of spiritual unity located in the papacy by the worldliness of many a Renaissance Pope.[17] Not even the rending of the religious unity of Christendom broke Western culture's basic dynamism, although by the time of the Enlightenment the resultant quarreling had occasioned the emergence of the ideal of tolerance as the supreme value in most Western countries and as the proper goal in questions of religion and culture.[18]

## Christendom, Tolerance and the New Evangelization

A crucial but often misunderstood aspect of the problem of religion and culture is the idea of "Christendom". Especially given Dawson's interest in the role of Christianity in the formation of Western culture, he could easily be taken as an apologist for the restoration of Christendom. But I do not believe that he was such, and I do not think that this is the direction of opportunity now at hand for the Church. It seems to be necessary to provide a different means for incorporating Christian principles into society than before. But merely to abandon the need for finding some real cultural embodiment of Christian principles is to leave oneself and society open to what has happened in the United States over the past generation. Human beings are social beings and are greatly influenced and affected as much or more by the customs of the society in which they live as by the ideas common to their era. Give up the work of structuring society according to religious principles, and you will expose the majority of people to the solicitations of grave evil.

Christendom is a term which suggests a dream long cherished, though always more a dream than a fact, a dream of a thorough integration of religion and politics in some form of theocracy. It was a dream sought in different ways by the competing papal and imperial parties in the era of the Holy

Roman Empire and the days of Pope Boniface VIII, with his claim to be able to seat and depose temporal rulers. It was a dream enacted for long periods in Spain, where alternate and interlocking authority gave kings the right to nominate bishops for papal appointment and the Church the right to direct the secular arm to work for forced conversions. One might say it was a Western dream that aspired to become like the Eastern Christianity of Byzantium.

But it was a dream that bred a certain amount of violence and forced conversions, a dream thoroughly disavowed by the Second Vatican Council, and not just there but progressively challenged by the Pian Popes in the sometimes reluctant but steady series of steps that have included the ceding of the Papal States and in the articulation of a prophetic social teaching by a series of encyclicals whose high moral road is possible in part because the Church has liberated herself from compromising temporal claims. In *The Judgement of the Nations* (1942) Dawson quotes at length from Pius XI's *Mit brennender Sorge* precisely on the relations between the common good and personal rights:

> The believer has an inalienable right to profess his faith and to practice it in the manner suited to him. Laws which suppress or render difficult the profession and practice of this faith are contrary to natural law (*Mit brennender Sorge* 35).

Dawson then comments on the strong affirmation of the right of religious freedom:

> This question has proved one of the stumbling blocks in the way of Christian co-operation . . . since it has been felt that Catholics have failed to recognize this principle. It is however clear from this passage . . . that on this particular issue there is no difference of opinion between Catholic and Protestant, and each is equally concerned to defend spiritual freedom against what Pius XI calls "the thousand forms of organized religious bondage," "the lack of truthful means and of the normal means of defence," . . . which are characteristic of the totalitarian state. . . .

It is clear to me that religious freedom is one of those "principles of human liberty and natural law. . . ." We must, however,
remember that the principles of natural law, essential as they are,
are only the minimal basis of common action. . . . No secular
remedy can meet the world's need; no purely moral effort can
restore true peace and spiritual order to society. The only final
end to which Christian action can be directed is the restoration
of all things in Christ. All Catholic teaching on social action
during the present century has been based on the doctrine of
the Universal Kingship of Christ, which is the Church's answer
to the universal claims of the totalitarian systems. But in spite
of its tremendous implications this doctrine should not be an
obstacle to Christian co-operation: it is a principle of unity, not
of division, for insofar as the Kingship of Christ is recognized
not as a theological abstraction but as a social reality, the divisions of Christendom will be transcended and the human race
will realize its organic unity under its Divine Head.[19]

Twenty years prior to the Vatican II declaration on religious
freedom, Dawson sees Pius XI as already articulating the personal right to religious freedom within a larger body of social
teaching ("principles of human liberty and natural law") and
sees this entire body of social teaching encompassed within the
evangelical mission of the Church to work for the Kingdom
of Christ. By gaining this perspective, one can transcend the
divisions that have torn apart Christendom and see the spiritual force that is the source of true unity—there is no talk of
a strategy to reconstitute Christendom politically.

This is to say that our saintly modern Popes have seen the
issue to be, *not the relation of Church and State, but the relation of
religion and culture.* The relation of Church and State has had
special meaning for American politics, where it is a matter of
no established or preferred religion (as the Anglican Church
had been the Established Church in mother England). In European politics the relation of Church and State suggests the
long-fought problem of investiture. But what the Popes have
tried to direct attention to is a different issue, *the relation of religion and culture*, and they have proved ever mindful, as Dawson

would put it, of "the intricate and far-reaching network of relations that unite the social way of life with the spiritual beliefs
and values which are accepted by society as the ultimate laws
of life and the ultimate stands of individual and social behavior."[20]

Whatever the technical problems with some of the specific
formulations of *Dignitatis humanæ*, the Vatican II Declaration
on Religious Freedom, a document like this shows a willingness to accommodate the modern liberal state and to use the
language of human rights just as Pius XI did.[21] It is not that
this form of social organization is privileged any more than
other forms with which the Church has had to deal, or that
the Church commits herself to it in preference to other forms
yet to be devised. But the document does contain a firm re-
pudiation of earlier insistence on a privileged position for the
Church, precisely so as to insist on the complete freedom of
the Church to evangelize and the right of individuals to worship God in freedom. Perhaps it is in response to the wars of
massive devastation and the swaggering presence of totalitarian
regimes for most of this century that prompted the Church at
this time to restate her perennial doctrines and aims in terms
of human dignity and personal responsibility.

We all know the sorry situation that perplexes the Church
when this document is read out of context, when some of its
phrases about the rights of the person to seek religious truth
according to his or her conscience are treated as if the document were promoting religious indifferentism instead of being
rightly interpreted with the Council's comments on evangelization. Some analysts consider the change of emphasis (from
"the rights of truth" in *Mirari vos* and *Lamentabile anni* to "the
rights of persons" in *Dignitatis humanæ*) to be a failure of nerve
and a capitulation to the secular ideal of tolerance. Granted,
the earlier formulations seem designed to prevent proselytizing
among Catholics by non-Catholics; but I wonder if the new
formulation was really not the product of far-sighted vision
of the pressing need to clear the decks for evangelical work,

a call to an evangelization that has still not yet fully found its voice. When we take the long historical perspective that Dawson recommends, the renewal of focus on reawakening evangelization rather than on reasserting the claims of Christendom seems to be precisely right. It is an effort to ready the Church for the struggles of the next century and the new millennium, with a better vision than any current political regime or national culture shows. Aware that the submerged religious roots of modern culture have been drying up, so much of the American Catholic subculture now dying and much of the missionary thrust of the Church withering away, the Church has been feeling her way toward taking the right steps and following the pattern of self-renewal that has been her mainstay these two millennia, the renewal of faith that will again animate cultural development.

On darker days one almost feels like asking, Will God permit the Church to die? But the answer is *no*. He may allow it to die in this or that part of Western culture, as he did in northern Africa after the glorious patristic age, and that would be a shame. The statistics on church-going in France, for instance, in Holland or in Scandinavia suggest it is already dead, except for the tiniest sprigs of green such as one sometimes sees on the edge of a tree stump.

But the clarity of the formal pronouncements of recent Popes and the Council on the fundamental dignity of the human person and on the need for direct and vigorous evangelization is corroborated for anyone with eyes to see in the experience of vigorous religious sects like the Mormons and Hispanic Pentecostals. One sees their lively church services, their young people happily committing part of their lives to the sole purpose of preaching and proselytizing; yet one also sees their weakness for lack of a principle of unity. There is much energy but little direction.

Our faith sustains the conviction that the Church will continue in our Lord's service. But the problem of how best to seek social embodiment of religious principles remains. Given the tremendous power government now has in all aspects of life, how do we resist the secularizing trends? If we stand aside on grounds that we are too pure to be involved in anything so mundane and possibly even as sordid as Church influence upon the State, we see the results in an administration whose very first executive orders were an attack on the unborn. Rather, the question is how our religious influence is to be exercised upon the State. Dawson's remarks from the very end of *Progress and Religion* may help to provide the necessary historical and sociological perspective:

> We have come to take it for granted that the unifying force in society is material interest, and that spiritual conviction is a source of strife and division. Modern civilization has pushed religion and the spiritual elements in culture out of the main stream of its development, so that they have lost touch with social life and have become sectarianized and impoverished. But at the same time this has led to the impoverishment of our whole culture. It has borne fruit in that "plebeianism of the European spirit" which Nietzsche regarded as the necessary consequence of the disappearance of the spiritual power. This, however, is but a temporary phenomenon; it can never be the normal condition of humanity. For, as we have seen, the vital and creative power behind every culture is a spiritual one. In proportion as the spiritual element recovers its natural position at the centre of our culture, it will necessarily become the mainspring of our whole social activity. This does not, however, mean that the material and spiritual aspects of life must become fused in a single political order which would have all the power and rigidity of a theocratic state. Since a culture is essentially a spiritual community, it transcends the economic and political orders. It finds its appropriate organ not in a state, but in a Church, that is to say a society which is the embodiment of a purely spiritual tradition and which rests, not on material power, but on the free adhesion of the individual mind. It has been the peculiar achievement of Western Christianity in the past to realize such an ideal in an organized spiritual society, which could co-exist with the national political units without either absorbing or being absorbed by them. The return to this tradition would once more make it

possible to reconcile the existence of national independence and
political freedom, which are an essential part of European life,
with the wider unity of our civilization, and with that higher
process of spiritual integration which is the true goal of human
progress. [22]

The crucial insight here, I think, is one that sets Dawson apart
from someone like his contemporary, T. S. Eliot. [23] Admittedly,
Eliot's earlier writings and his poems, like the Choruses from
*The Rock*, show him to be Christian in his sympathies. But
his later letters reveal his admiration for religion merely as a
matrix of culture. This reverses their order of importance. It is
almost as though he valued Christianity because it produced
the kind of culture he admired. Dawson, on the other hand,
seems to me to be clearer about the importance of a social
embodiment of religious principles so as to serve the genuine
aims of religion, the better to allow free persons rightly to order their relations to their God and their fellow creatures.

That Dawson stands for keeping a spiritual force alive and
vigorous in culture, and not for a return to Christendom, is
clear in yet another way from his educational writings and especially, *The Crisis of Western Education*. Recognizing as he does
the crucial nature of the control of education in the present cultural conflict, he does not urge a defensive fight to reestablish
some cherished status quo, even the traditional humanist education in the Latin and Greek classics. Instead he proposes an
innovation much in the spirit of his general view of the relation
of religion and culture, namely, making the study of Christian
culture the center of a curriculum. He envisions this proposal
not just as an alternative but an antidote to the "combination
of utilitarianism and specialism [which] is not only fatal to the
idea of a liberal education, [but] is also one of the main causes
of the intellectual disintegration of modern Western culture."
Commenting on the increasingly technological cast of our society, Dawson alerts us to a paradox: the promissory character
of technological materialism (where the answer to all problems
is forever promised in the future by some technical solution,

without need for responsible use of our freedom) has had the effect of alienating the great mass of men and women from nature, from one another and even from reality itself. His proposal to make the study of the dynamic relations of religion and culture central to the curriculum seems intended to restore a sense of historical reality over against the hedonistic delusions of postmodern "virtual reality". Without making religion into a rationalized system of conclusions, the historical approach can assist the work of evangelization by providing an organized matrix for study and for asking questions about the importance of spiritual reality in various cultures at various periods of their development.

## Conclusion

The optimism that marks Dawson's vision is neither promissory materialism nor the weary old religion of progress, but the virtue of hope. In my judgment, this is the supernatural gift needed for the work toward which a proper understanding of the relation of religion and culture points. Thankfully, there is much evidence that the Church—once again and still, as always—envisions direct evangelization as her most proper task. How and when the fruit will come is not ours to see. But in *The Historic Reality of Christian Culture* Dawson reminds us of the way this hope succeeds:

> The remaking of an old culture by the birth of a new hope was not the conscious aim of the Christians themselves. They tended, like St. Cyprian, to believe that the world was growing old, that the empire was irremediably pagan and that some world catastrophe was imminent. Nevertheless they lived in a spiritual atmosphere of hope, and this atmosphere gradually spread until the climate of the world was changed. The heartless, hopeless Rome which found its monstrous expression in the Colosseum and the gladiatorial games became the Rome of St. Leo and St. Gregory—a city which laid the foundations of a new world

while its own world was falling in ruin around it. We see the same process at work in northern Europe during the Dark Ages. The men who converted the warrior peoples of the north and laid the foundations of medieval culture had no conception of the new world they were creating and no belief in the temporal future of civilization. But they were men of hope, as they were men of faith, and therefore their work endured for a thousand years and bore rich fruit in every field of cultural activity, as well as on its own religious level.[24]

# NOTES

[1] Christopher Dawson, *The Gods of Revolution: An Analysis of the French Revolution*, introduction by Arnold Toynbee (New York: Minerva Press, 1972, 1975), and *The Spirit of the Oxford Movement* (London: Sheed & Ward, 1934).

[2] Christopher Dawson, *Religion and Culture*. Gifford Lectures delivered in the University of Edinburgh, 1947–1948 (London: Sheed & Ward, 1948), p. 50.

[3] Ibid., p. 50.

[4] Christopher Dawson, *Religion and the Rise of Western Culture*. Gifford Lectures delivered in the University of Edinburgh, 1948–1949 (London: Sheed & Ward, 1950; Garden City, N.Y.: Doubleday Image, 1958), p. 19.

[5] In *Modern Times: The World from the Twenties to the Eighties* (New York: Harper & Row, 1983), Paul Johnson gives repeated examples of the sorry experience of young developing nations which got only a parasitical class of professional politicians who pocketed Western funding and appropriated the name "democracy" instead of some actual system of fairness and timely justice and the basic stability needed for economic growth, a vision that has been associated with the ideal called "democracy" that the Third World has found so enticing.

[6] See, e.g., chapter 7, "The Secularization of Western Culture and the Rise of the Religion of Progress", in Christopher Dawson's *Progress and Religion* (London: Sheed & Ward, 1929, but recently reprinted by Sherwood Sugden & Co., June 1992).

[7] This has been noticed by authors in both the conservative and liberal spheres. See Benedict J. Groeschel, C.F.R., *The Reform of Renewal* (San Francisco: Ignatius Press, 1990), and Patricia Wittberg, S.C., *Creating a Future for Religious Life: A Sociological Perspective* (Mahwah, N.J.: Paulist Press, 1991). For background discussion, see Avery Dulles, S.J., *Models of the Church* (New York: Doubleday, 1974).

[8] Pope John Paul II has repeatedly called for a "new evangelization". Throughout his Pontificate he has sounded the religion and cultural theme, e.g., during his 1982 pilgrimage to Santiago de Compostela, when he urged Europe to be "the beacon of civilization" (cf. *The New York Times*, Wednesday, November 10, 1992). In 1982 he established the Pontifical Council on Culture to promote his own humanistic theory of culture.

[9] See Dawson's comments on this doctrine in "St. Augustine and the City of God" in his *The Dynamics of World History*, edited by John J. Mulloy (LaSalle, Ill.: Sherwood Sugden & Co., 1978), pp. 294–325.

[10] Dawson finds the only prolonged exception to this in Western culture to be the Carolingian Empire, which attempted to impose theocratic rule in oriental style; even as it faltered, it gave birth to the Church-State problem that for a thousand years dominated the question of the relation of religion and culture. See Dawson, *Religion and the Rise of Western Culture*, pp. 62–66, 84–85 and 90–91. For comparison with the theocratic regime in Byzantium, see pp. 104–6.

[11] See Dawson, *Religion and Culture*, p. 53.

[12] Christopher Dawson, *The Judgement of the Nations* (New York: Sheed & Ward, 1942), pp. 22–24.

[13] Christopher Dawson, *Christianity and the New Age* (London: Sheed & Ward, 1931), pp. 94–96.

[14] Dawson, *Religion and the Rise of Western Culture*, pp. 16–17.

[15] Ibid., pp. 18–19.

[16] Ibid., p. 19. For the details, see chapters 2–5.

[17] See Dawson, *The Dividing of Christendom* (New York: Sheed & Ward, 1965).

[18] Cf. Dawson, *The Judgement of the Nations*, pp. 64–65: "It was in England in the 17th century that the Christian ideal of spiritual freedom and the medieval tradition of political liberties came together to produce the new liberal ideology which was the main inspiration for Western civilization for more than two centuries and out of which political liberalism in the strict sense finally developed. The failure of liberalism in the course of the last century has been due above all to the failure of the liberal parties to give adequate expression to this ideology and to the still deeper social tradition that lies behind it. The liberal movement in the wider sense transformed the world by an immense liberation of human energies, but liberalism in the narrower sense proved incapable of guiding the forces that it had realized. It became a negative and defensive creed which from the socialist standpoint represented nothing more than class interest."

[19] Ibid., pp. 166–68.

[20] Dawson, *Religion and the Rise of Western Culture*, p. 12.

[21] Unfortunately, the Christian origins of the theory of human rights is generally neglected by enthusiasts of the Enlightenment. A trustworthy account of the notion of natural rights and its parent notion natural law is to be found in Yves R. Simon's *The Tradition of Natural Law: A Philosopher's Reflections* (New York: Fordham University Press, 1965, 1992). While Jacques Maritain can also be credited with trying to bring out the Christian origins of the modern theory of human rights, the subtitle of his masterwork on the subject gives us pause: *Integral Humanism: Temporal and Spiritual Problems of a New Christendom*, translated by Joseph W. Evans (French original, 1936; Charles Scribner's Sons, 1968).

[22] *Progress and Religion*, pp. 249–50.

[23] See Dawson's essay, "T. S. Eliot on the Meaning of Culture", in *The Dynamics of World History*, pp. 103–10.

[24] Christopher Dawson, *The Historic Reality of Christian Culture*, p. 65.

ROBERT V. YOUNG

# NATURE AND GRACE IN
# THE CHARACTER OF WESTERN MAN

"I just don't get it." These are the plaintive words of syndicated columnist Ellen Goodman, and her chagrin arises from the persistent reports of unseemly sexual antics on the part of Senator Robert Packwood that were making the news toward the end of 1992. "I don't understand", Ms. Goodman moans, "how a senator like Bob Packwood, who used his power to help women succeed as equals in public life, apparently also used his power to take advantage of them in private life." She is so frustrated that an explanation is sought in amateur neurology: "What synapse misfires in a character who make[s] advances for women and then also makes 'unwanted sexual advances' on women? What part of the electrical system simply disconnects?" What is even more unsettling to the columnist is the observation, which she quotes from Constance Buchanan of the Harvard Divinity School, that "good guys do this all the time." To paraphrase the title of a tawdry novel of some years ago, poor Ms. Goodman is, rather forlornly, looking for Mr. Good Guy.[1]

The status of "good guy" has been conferred upon Senator Packwood and his ilk largely because they are supporters of legalized abortion, although "Any number of women will attest to the fact", Ms. Goodman avers, "that Packwood was genuinely supportive of their professional success." Only in the hothouse world of contemporary feminism would anyone assume that a man's willingness to help women procure abortions or make money would also indicate a tender regard for their

37

dignity and delicacy of feeling. Abortion is, after all, chiefly a means of eliminating the unintended and inconvenient consequences of recreational eroticism; if a woman enjoys sufficient "professional success" to pay for her own—so much the better. Men who are avid supporters of equality for women are all too often little more than equal-opportunity adulterers.

Now the perplexity of an Ellen Goodman over what she perceives as the "contradictions" in the character of a man like Robert Packwood has implications that extend beyond the specific issue of abortion, beyond even the murky controversy over the proper relationship between the sexes. At stake is the nature of individual character and the mode in which it is constituted in relation to culture. The current confusion, not only in the popular media but also in the academy, over what makes a "good guy" grows out of a misapprehension about the interaction of character and culture and about the limits inherent in both. In book after book, Christopher Dawson emphasizes the uniquely dynamic nature of Western culture; that is, the capacity of European Christendom to develop in unforeseen ways and to extend itself throughout the world in recent centuries. "Western civilization has been the great ferment of change in the world," Dawson writes, "because changing the world became an integral part of its cultural ideal."[2] This factor of change is both the promise and the peril of Western culture, because it complicates the essential function of any culture as such:

> But the real unity of culture is not to be found in blood or soil or economic class and function. Each of these factors has its importance, but none of them suffice[s] to explain the inner nature of a culture. In addition to all these elements of partial community, a culture is also a moral order and involves a community of values and standards which provide its internal or moral principle of unity.[3]

A culture that incorporates "change in the world" as a principle is, therefore, a daunting proposition in view of the central role that it plays in the moral unity of society.

The notion seems even more problematic when Dawson's concept of the relation between culture and the individual person is taken into account:

> Culture is the name which has been given to man's social inheritance—to all that men have learnt from the past by the process of imitation, education and learning and to all that they hand on in like manner to their descendants and successors. And this involves all that man has and is. For if it were possible to separate an individual altogether from his culture and his social inheritance, he would be an idiot, living in a private world of formless feelings, but lower than the beasts, since he would no longer possess the guidance of instinct which is the basis of animal behavior.[4]

Given the moral *idiocy* that seems pervasive in the current American scene, one might infer that a mass alienation of individuals from their culture had occurred; and in fact such a description would not be wholly inaccurate. It seems that in contemporary Western society change has become virtually an end in itself, so that we have a kind of "anti-culture", which negates the unitary purpose of culture as such. The result is that we are all, in some measure, "idiots"—estranged from our fellow citizens, uncertain of how to behave or what to believe, abandoned in a wilderness of meaninglessness.

It may be that we are witnesses to the disintegration of a culture and a moral order two thousand years and more in the making. It is no less true for being a truism that Western civilization represents the convergence of Athens and Jerusalem, of classical philosophy and Judaeo-Christian revelation, of nature and grace. As the privileged heir to this tradition, Western man has, for several centuries, tended to take it for granted and, more recently, to despise it altogether. We now confront a generation for many of whom the traditional culture of the West is simply incomprehensible. The dynamic character of Western culture, noted by Dawson, lies precisely in the nexus of nature and grace: in the transfiguration of what is naturally human by divine favor. The divine half of the equation was put in question by the Reformation and has been increasingly neglected or denied in the wake of the Enlightenment; in our era even human nature has been rendered problematic. As long as some sense of natural norms or standards persists, then at least the possibility of grace is implicit precisely in the inevitable failure of human beings to attain what seems to be the fulfillment of their natural birthright; but once this sense of nature is lost, then there can be no conception of the grace that transcends it.

The current dismantling of Western culture can be witnessed in two quite diverse but equally fundamental areas of human life: sex and language. Both instances provide evidence of the reciprocal deleterious effects of the vicious behavior of individuals on the health of a culture and of the moral decline of a culture upon the character of individuals. Christopher Dawson observes, in "The Patriarchal Family in History", that normative sexuality is necessary to the very existence of civilization: "It is impossible to go back behind the family and find a state of society in which sexual relations are in a presocial stage, for the regulation of sexual relations is an essential prerequisite of any kind of culture." In this 1933 essay, Dawson proceeds to express alarm over the prospect of a general acceptance of contraception in the Western world and its effect upon the family: "Marriage will lose all of its attractions for the young and the pleasure loving and the poor and the ambitious. The energy of youth will be devoted to contraceptive love and only when men and women have become prosperous and middle-aged will they think seriously of settling down to rear a strictly limited family."[5] Dawson also maintains that language is an integral feature of human culture: "Culture and language are inseparable aspects of the same process, so that it is impossible to regard one of them as existing without the other." This linguistic element is the decisive factor in man's capacity to perceive reality: "Thus a culture and its language taken together", Dawson continues, "form an autonomous world of meaning and existence which is indeed the only world of which the individual is conscious."[6] Even with his prescience it seems unlikely that Dawson could have foreseen the extent to which his worst fears would be realized by the 1990s.

In an essay recently published in *Crisis*, "Judaism's Sexual Revolution: Why Judaism Rejected Homosexuality", Dennis Prager takes up Dawson's theme in specific and absolute terms: "When Judaism demanded that all sexual activity be channeled into marriage, it changed the world. The Torah's prohibition of non-marital sex quite simply made the creation of Western civilization possible."[7] Prager emphasizes the radical novelty, the uniqueness of the Judaeo-Christian sexual ethic, ascribing it to the superiority of revealed wisdom over human reasoning. His studies of the pervasiveness of homosexuality have convinced him that heterosexual monogamy is necessarily the fruit of divine revelation: "The Torah is simply too different from the rest of the world, too against man's nature, to have been solely man-made."[8]

Prager's insight is important, but it requires qualification. I am especially bothered by the notion that revelation is simply "against man's nature". Much is made of the pervasiveness of pedophilia in ancient Greek culture, and Plato's attachment to this vice is often cited. Such a view of Plato can come only of a superficial reading, neglectful of his typical genre, which is dialogue not treatise. The *Symposium*, for example, is an account of a drinking party among a group of artists and intellectuals where all the participants agree to make speeches in praise of Love (i.e., the god, Eros). Except for Socrates all the speakers give elaborate defenses of pederasty, but the speeches are so extravagant that they betray a certain uneasiness on the part of the speakers, and sometimes the underlying disapproval of Athenian society emerges, as in these remarks of the physician, Pausanias:

> . . . one would have thought that, here if anywhere, loving and being kind to one's lover would have been positively applauded. Yet we find in practice that if a father discovers that someone has fallen in love with his son, he puts the boy in charge of an attendant, with strict injunctions not to let him have anything

to do with his lover. And if the boy's little friends and playmates see anything of that kind going on, you may be sure they'll call him names, while their elders will neither stop their being rude nor tell them they are talking nonsense (183c).[9]

Much the same tone of vexed superiority is adopted toward ordinary respectable society by many of today's "gay" spokesmen, and the negative response toward homosexuality, typical even of Athenian society, is reflected by Plato's *Phædrus* in the speech of the sophist Lysias, who admonishes a young man to accept the advances not of a lover but of a "nonlover", because the latter will keep the sexual relationship secret and avoid the disapproval of the youth's friends and relatives (232a–b, 234b).[10] Of course both dialogues end with speeches by Socrates, exhorting his hearers to rise above physical love altogether and to channel the energy of Eros into the ascent of the ladder of love, which leads to contemplation of the Ideas.

The example of Plato suggests not that man's nature is simply and unequivocally licentious, but that his idealistic aspirations —the speakers in the *Symposium* all wish to see love as an exalted spiritual experience—are almost inevitably frustrated and perverted. The Roman poet Catullus provides another compelling witness from classical literature. One of his epithalamia (or wedding hymns) suggests both the indecencies that pagan Rome seems to have taken for granted and also a certain discomfort with such licentiousness. The groom's boy lover (*concubinus*) is adjured not to deny nuts to the children upon hearing that his master has abandoned his love (scattering nuts in the wake of the procession was traditional at Roman weddings), and the groom is admonished to overcome his reluctance to surrender the boy's favors:

> It is said, anointed groom,
> That you hardly keep yourself
> Away from your hairless boys,
> But keep away.

> We are aware that things
> Known to you are only what
> Are permitted pleasures,
> But the same things are not allowed
> To husbands.[11]

To be sure, this passage is Catullus' imitation of the "Fescennine verses" that were the bawdy abuse of the groom conventional at Roman weddings. Nevertheless, while one is loath to speculate about what pleasures were *not* permitted, there is a clear sense that the pervasive pederasty was regarded as unseemly and certainly unsuitable for a married man even among the Romans who tolerated it.

The same anguished and divided consciousness is apparent in Catullus' most famous poems, the love lyrics written to and about one "Lesbia", which seem to reflect an actual adulterous affair with the disreputable Clodia excoriated in Cicero's *Pro Cælio*. The poems blend passionate ardor, withering obscenity and despairing disillusionment: a mixture that a Christian might take as the faint but painful stirring of a woefully unformed conscience. Many of the poems express this agonized ambivalence, but perhaps the following is the most poignant:

> Formerly you used to say that Catullus alone
>     Was intimate with you, Lesbia, that you
> Would not have Jove instead of me.
>     I cherished you then not only as the crowd
> Loves a girlfriend, but as a father loves
>     His sons and sons-in-law. Now I know you:
> Hence even if I burn more extravagantly, to me
>     You are cheaper and looser. How so? you ask.
> Because such a wound compels a lover
>     To love with more desire but less good will.[12]

The poem displays a powerful negative eloquence in revealing the poet's struggle to express what is for him inexpressible. "The reader can sense Catullus here searching for terms which will give force to the selflessness of the emotion he feels," writes Gordon Williams, "and here he finds them in the Roman

sense of family and the ties that hold it together."[13] Catullus is
determined to regard his affair with Lesbia as something more
than a mere adulterous "fling": his bitterness over her "be-
trayal", her refusal to see it in his terms, is a measure of the
significance with which the poet seeks to invest his passion.
Thus in another poem he prays that gods bring Lesbia the will
to maintain "this eternal pact of sacred friendship" (CIX.6:
"æternum hoc sanctæ fœdus amicitiæ"), and in yet another
he justifies himself against her because he "has never violated
a sacred vow, nor in any pact / abused the power of the gods
for deceiving men" (LXXVI.3–4: "nec sanctum violasse fi-
dem, nec fœdere in ullo / divum ad fallendos numine abusum
homines").

The kind of mutual love longed for by Catullus, desperately
sought through intimacy with a courtesan or another man's
faithless wife, would only become possible with the Christian
transformation of marriage. Christopher Dawson points out
that the patriarchal family could not survive the cultural disintegration of the classical world known to Catullus:

> Conditions of life both in the Greek city state and in the Roman
> Empire favoured the man without a family who could devote
> his whole energies to the duties and pleasures of public life.
> Late marriages and small families became the rule, and men
> satisfied their sexual instincts by homosexuality or by relations
> with slaves and prostitutes. This aversion to marriage and the
> deliberate restriction of the family by the practice of infanticide
> and abortion was undoubtedly the main cause of the decline
> of ancient Greece, as Polybius pointed out in the second cen-
> tury B.C.[14]

The parallels with contemporary postindustrial societies present disturbing prospects for our future, but, as Dawson argues
further, the alternative has already been established in Christianity's elevation of the patriarchal family to a higher plane:

> While the patriarchal family in its original form was an aris-
> tocratic institution which was the privilege of a ruling race or

patrician class, the Christian family was common to every class, even to the slaves. Still more important was the fact that the Church insisted for the first time on the mutual and bilateral character of sexual obligations. The husband belonged to the wife as exclusively as the wife to the husband. This rendered marriage a more personal and individual relation than it had been under the patriarchal system.[15]

The longing of Catullus, who died half a century before the birth of Christ, was thus fulfilled among a people whom he would have despised had he troubled to notice them.

St. Augustine can hardly be regarded as a liberal, much less as a sentimentalist, about marriage, but he, nevertheless, finds a good in Christian marriage as such that fulfills the longing expressed by Catullus:

> It does not seem to me that [the good of marriage] is on account of the procreation of children alone, but also on account of the society natural to the diversity of sexes. Otherwise it could not be called marriage among the aged, especially if they either had lost their children or had generated none at all. But in a good marriage, although of many years, even if the fire of youth has cooled between the man and woman, still the order of charity thrives between the husband and wife.

Even in the time of "youthful incontinence", St. Augustine continues, "concupiscence of the flesh, which is tempered by parental affection, burns in a somewhat more moderate fashion because it is restrained. For a certain gravity intervenes in the fervid pleasure, when a man and woman cleaving to one another consider being a father and mother."[16]

What is more, Christianity introduced into the institution the element of sacramental mystery, transcending anything conceived of marriage within pagan culture:

> But since out of many souls there is to be one city of those having one soul and one heart in God (Acts 4.32), which will be the perfection of our unity after this pilgrimage, where the thoughts of all will not be hidden from each other, nor among

themselves will they be at odds in anything: consequently the sacrament of marriage is in our time confined to one man and one wife. . . .[17]

The ultimate source of Augustine's view of Christian marriage is the "great mystery" (*Sacramentum hoc magnum est*) of Ephesians 5:32, by which the wedding of an individual man and woman becomes a sign of the bond between Christ and his Church. It is this great dignity that distinguishes Christian from pagan marriage and makes the former a channel of grace. "The good of marriage among all nations and all men is, then, for the sake of generation and the vow of chastity", Augustine writes; "however, what also pertains to the people of God is in the holiness of the Sacrament."[18]

This elevation of marriage is a fundamental element in the development of the character of Western man, and it is a perfect example of the convergence of nature and grace, of Athens and Jerusalem. The proud pagans, Plato and Catullus, had sensed and responded to the emptiness in the human soul, to the failure of Eros: surely that urgent, fiery energy in man's nature should culminate in something more than the spasmodic conquest of a hairless boy or a faithless woman? The fulfillment of this natural craving, however, comes only in the order of grace: "Thou hast hid these things from the wise and prudent and hast revealed them to little ones" (Mt 11:25). The surrender to grace, to the holiness of the sacrament, the giving of oneself wholly to one other person on the part of the man as well as the woman, is what makes of Christian marriage, in Dawson's words, "a more personal and individual relation". Or, as Augustine says, it allows *ardor* to open into the *order* of charity. It enables the kind of relationship that Catullus desired, but it requires a different kind of man—a man of patience and humility. And here the influence of Christian culture on the character of Western man is quite apparent.

While sexuality is one element in human life that ties us to the earth and proclaims our kinship with the beasts that perish, language is evidence of our distinctive rationality. The capacity for speech and writing is our most powerful and supple means of apprehending and deploying signs and symbols in the construction of meaning; it is the manifestation and instrument of our self-awareness. For this reason Dawson regards language as "inseparable" from culture: they are coextensive factors in the shaping of human identity both individually and communally. Now as the preeminent sign system, language reveals most clearly the paradox of signification: signs mean what they are not. The result is that knowledge and understanding, mediated by language, abstract and alienate mankind from their objects. The problematic status of language has been increasingly insisted upon as the twentieth century has proceeded, but Plato was aware of the limitations of language, and St. Augustine even more acutely so.[19]

If the problem of language has grown especially troublesome in our age—as sex has—it is because we have, again, neglected the solution that has already been discovered. It is a solution that arises, again, in the convergence of Athens and Jerusalem. As Christopher Dawson points out, "when St. Paul appealed to the testimony of the Stoic poet, he recognized that Christianity was prepared to accept the metaphysical inheritance of Hellenistic thought as well as the historic revelation of Jewish prophecy." The dilemma of classical philosophy lies in the chasm that opens up between the ideal metaphysical structures of the intellect and the mutable physical realm in which human beings dwell. It is no wonder that Hellenic philosophy is so often tinged with despair and advocates, implicitly or explicitly, a withdrawal from the common earthly existence of mankind. "St. John's identification of the Logos and the Messiah", offers, as Dawson observes, a way out of this dilemma:

> Jesus of Nazareth was not only the Christ, the Son of the Living God; He was also the Divine Intelligence, the Principle of the order and intelligibility of the created world. Thus the opposition between the Greek ideal of spiritual intuition and the Living God of Jewish revelation—an opposition that Philo had vainly

attempted to surmount by an artificial philosophic synthesis—
finally disappeared before the revelation of the Incarnate Word.[20]

"Incarnate Word" is a paradox that baffles the unaided, unregenerate human intellect, "a stone of offense and a rock of
stumbling" (1 Pet 2:8: "et lapis offensionis, et petra scandali");
but this central Christian paradox is the channel of the grace
that binds our errant souls to reality. As our words represent
(re-present) the link between our knowledge and our world,
so the Word made flesh is the Presence of meaning and order
within temporal actuality. Or in the phrasing of Christopher
Dawson, drawing upon St. Augustine:

> Jesus is the bridge between Humanity and Divinity. In Him
> God is not only manifested to man, but vitally participated. He
> is the Divine Life, which transforms human nature and makes
> it the partaker of Its own supernatural activity.[21]

The Incarnate Word is thus the poetry of human existence,
finding its most powerful manifestation in the Church's liturgical appropriation of the Psalter. The undoubted excellence of
Greco-Roman poetry notwithstanding, there is, Dawson maintains, a unique superiority in the Christian liturgy:

> This was new poetry indeed. It expressed what had never been
> expressed in classical poetry and it expressed it in a new lan-
> guage and a new rhythm. Nevertheless it became immediately
> popular with the Gentile converts as well as with Jewish Chris-
> tians. It expressed spiritual things with a much greater intensity
> and with more intense personal feeling than classical poetry had
> ever attained, even in a narrower range and on a lower level. It
> was a poetry which could be applied by the individual Christian
> to express his own thoughts and feelings, yet it was at the same
> time the voice of the Church and the voice of Christ. . . .[22]

I would suggest that the key to the difference between classical and Christian poetry can be found in the word "liturgy",
which ultimately derives from the Greek *leitourgia*—the perfor-
mance of public service for the State or the gods. This means
that the utterance of the language of the liturgy is not just

saying, it is doing; it is a work undertaken and carried out and, as such, plays a part in shaping the character of its participants. "The conscious, fully awakened act of performing the Liturgy", remarks Dietrich von Hildebrand, "imprints upon the soul the Face of Christ. In taking part in the Liturgy, we make our own the fundamental attitudes embodied in it."[23]

"Hence the insistence of the Fourth Gospel", Dawson writes, "on the sacramental element in Christ's teaching, since it is through the sacraments that the Incarnation of the Divine Word is no longer merely a historical fact, but is brought into vital and sensible contact with the life of the believer."[24] In the sacraments words do not merely represent; they make present. In the celebration of the Mass, Christians share in the present reality of the divine life, and this develops an altogether new, grace-filled character in the humanity of Christendom. What is more, the supernaturally charged language of the liturgy enables mankind to see the world in terms of a new vision. Language has meaning in a new way because things themselves have meaning in a new way: "Let your spirit wander through the entire creation," Augustine says, "and everywhere the creation will cry out to you: God made me."[25] And writing on the same verse of the Psalms (26:6), Cardinal Bellarmine remarks, "Therefore the Prophet, exalted through contemplation upon all earthly things, breaks out in admiration of the works of God, and praise of the almighty workman."[26] In other words, the world shaped by the divine Logos of the one God of Abraham, Isaac and Jacob is a different place from a world ruled by an arbitrary and impersonal necessity and haunted by an array of capricious "gods" and demons.

It is faith in the one God, whose only Son is both the informing principle and Redeemer of the world, that has made possible the distinctive character of Western man—a character marked by optimism based ultimately on hope, hope in what we do not see (Romans 8:24–25). The corruption of our nature that results not only in sin but also in failures of vision and confusion of meaning can be purified by grace. It is for this reason that the definitive works of classical literature are tragic, but the greatest work of Christendom is the Divine Comedy. The Enlightenment concept of progress, a debased and secularized version of Christian hope, could only have emerged within a decaying Christendom. With what seems to be the final collapse of the Western world's belief in material progress, it would seem that our only hope is hope; that is, the theological virtue. "The day of the Liberal Deist compromise is over," Christopher Dawson pointed out some sixty years ago, "and we have come to the parting of the ways. Either Europe must abandon the Christian tradition and with it the faith in progress and humanity, or it must return consciously to the religious foundation on which these ideas were based."[27]

It seems rather painfully clear that the Western world, at least as represented by its most influential and prestigious individuals and institutions, has chosen to abandon progress and humanity along with Christianity. There would seem to be no other explanation for the sordid tale that opens this paper. Only breathtaking naïveté would find anything surprising in the report that a powerful, affluent man had attempted to use his position to exploit women sexually: we are all acquainted with the stories of David and Bathsheba and Susannah among the elders. What is disturbing is that the Senator has expressed regret, not for a lack of integrity or for immoral conduct, but a misunderstanding—presumably he means that he misjudged the intentions of the women, that adultery would have been acceptable between "consenting adults". Even more disturbing is the way that Ellen Goodman, who undertakes to speak for the victims, shrugs off the behavior of a scoundrel as a failure in the nervous system and still accords him, however ruefully, the title of "good guy", because he votes the party line on "women's issues". Although she insists that powerful men "have to change", the change will come, not of improved character, but of increased feminist political pressure.

Christian culture in its essence is a culture of hope; we are witnesses in our generation to its displacement by a culture of despair. Despite the ravages of original sin, the Christian always has hope in the profusion of grace poured out with the blood of Jesus shed on Calvary. Through this grace, the image of God can always be restored in the countenance of fallen man, be it ever so twisted and pock-marked by sin. The history of Christendom, like that of humanity in general, is for the most part shabby: a record of cruelty and violence, shame and vice; but it is recurrently illuminated by unforeseen acts of courage, kindness and decency among ordinary men and women and transfigured by the lives of the saints. Of course such evidence of the work of Christ's abundant grace and mercy in the world has not ceased, but it no longer counts among our cultural elites and dominant institutions. This state of affairs has been developing for centuries, as Christopher Dawson observes:

> So we have the paradox that at the beginning of the Renaissance, when the conquest of nature and the creation of modern science are still unrealized, man appears in god-like freedom with a sense of unbounded power and greatness; while at the end of the nineteenth century, when nature has been conquered and there seem no limits to the powers of science, man is once more conscious of his misery as the slave of material circumstance and physical appetite and death.[28]

In a recent article in *First Things*, Robert W. Jensen has suggested that the postmodern world—the cultural void that attends upon the disintegration of modernism—is a world in which stories cannot be true and promises cannot be kept. Promises make no sense in a world without a coherent narrative, without a story; and there can, finally, be no meaningful story without a Storyteller. Postmodernism is merely the culmination of the modern world's effort to banish God from his creation.[29] At the center of the nihilistic vortex that has whirled through academic life in recent years is the analytic method called deconstruction, which explicitly sets out to drain the meaning out of any text from within by an act of expropriation, by inhabiting it as a parasite. The principal goal of deconstruction, if the term "goal" is appropriate in such a context, is to discredit and dismantle what is called "logocentric metaphysics" or "ontotheology"—in other words, God, especially the Second Person of the Trinity, conceived as the agent of reason, order and meaning in the world. Now deconstruction is a very esoteric theory, and I am routinely assured by colleagues that it is already out of fashion; but I find no solace in such assurances. If deconstruction has truly become passé in the realm of scholarship, that is only because it has made so complete a conquest of popular culture. "We should turn from elite art to the streets of our cities and the classrooms of our suburbs", Jensen remarks (p. 21).

My own experience in the university classroom tends to confirm this admonition: for vast numbers—perhaps for a majority—of the current generation of college students, sexual intercourse is a negotiable "relationship" for the purpose of mutual "fulfillment of needs", music is a stream of shouted threats and obscenities with deafening electronic accompaniment, "Madonna" is only the name of a pop singer whose chief distinction is to behave like a prostitute in various entertainment media, and high art consists largely of films saturated with vulgar cynicism, frenzied violence and sexual perversion. We are, then, witnessing the fulfillment of Dawson's darkest prophecies:

> We have entered a new phase of culture—we may call it the Age of the Cinema—in which the most amazing perfection of scientific technique is being devoted to purely ephemeral objects, without any consideration of their ultimate justification. It seems as though a new society was arising which will acknowledge no hierarchy of values, no intellectual authority, and no social or religious tradition, but which will live for the moment in a chaos of pure sensation.[30]

Perhaps even Dawson would be astounded to see how rapidly his prediction of "social disintegration" attendant upon such a state of affairs would come to pass. Could even he have envisioned a 25 percent illegitimacy rate despite more than a million and a half abortions per year, soaring rates of rape and child abuse, neighborhoods paralyzed by drug addiction and drive-by shootings, metal detectors at the entrances of high schools and condom distribution to school children by public authorities?

The character of Western man was created by the emergence of Christian culture, and the modern world has lived off the Christian heritage even while repudiating it. The accumulated moral capital now seems wholly squandered, and the world itself has no prospect of renewing it—fallen man is without resources of his own. There is, however, as Dawson points out, an infinite, unfailing source of restoration in the grace of Christ:

> Every Christian mind is a seed of change so long as it is a living mind, not enervated by custom or ossified by prejudice. A Christian has only to *be* in order to change the world, for in that act of being there is contained all the mystery of supernatural life. It is the function of the Church to sow this divine seed, to produce not merely good men, but spiritual men—that is to say, supermen. Insofar as the Church fulfills this function it transmits to the world a continuous stream of spiritual energy. If the salt itself loses its savor, then indeed the world sinks back into disorder and death, for a despiritualized Christianity is powerless to change anything; it is the most abject of failures, since it serves neither the natural nor the spiritual order.[31]

Men and women can become good citizens and good neighbors again only by becoming something more, by recovering the grace of Christ Jesus. By the same token, the Church can influence society in a positive way, not by becoming merely another social service agency or political pressure group, but by proclaiming the gospel and celebrating the sacraments—by serving as a channel of grace. We must remember that nature is never enough, that the world cannot even be itself unless it is infused with heaven. On the realization that civilization is insufficient, the fate of civilization rests.

# NOTES

[1] Goodman's column, "Men in Power Have to Change", syndicated by the Boston *Globe*, is quoted from the Raleigh *News & Observer*, December 4, 1992.

[2] *Religion and the Rise of Western Culture* (1950; reprint, Garden City, N.Y.: Doubleday Image, 1958), p. 17.

[3] Christopher Dawson, *The Formation of Christendom* (New York: Sheed & Ward, 1967), p. 44.

[4] Ibid., p. 31.

[5] *The Dynamics of World History*, ed. John J. Mulloy (LaSalle, Ill.: Sherwood Sugden & Co., 1978), pp. 157–58, 165.

[6] *The Formation of Christendom*, pp. 35–36.

[7] *Crisis* 11, no. 8 (September 1993), p. 29.

[8] Ibid., p. 36.

[9] Trans. Michael Joyce, in *Plato: The Collected Dialogues*, ed. Edith Hamilton and Huntington Cairns, Bollingen Series LXXI (Princeton, N.J.: Princeton University Press, 1961), p. 537.

[10] Trans. R. Hackforth, *Collected Dialogues*, pp. 480–82.

[11] Catullus, *Carmina* LXI.137–39, 142–44. The translation is made from the Latin text of the Loeb Library edition, ed. and trans. F. W. Cornish, rev. ed. (Cambridge: Harvard University Press, 1962), pp. 76, 78: "diceris male te a tuis / unguentate glabris, marite, abstinere: sed abstine. . . . scimus hæc tibi quæ licent / sola cognita: sed marito / ista non eadem licent."

[12] Ibid., LXXII, p. 152: "Dicebas quondam solum te nosse Catullum, / Lesbia, nec præ me velle tenere Iovem. / dilexi tum te non tantum ut vulgus amicam, / sed pater ut gnatos diligit et generos. / nunc te cognovi: quare etsi impensius uror, / multo mi tamen es vilior et levior. / qui potis est? inquis. quod amantem iniuria talis / cogit amare magis, sed bene velle minus."

[13] *The Nature of Roman Poetry* (New York: Oxford University Press, 1983), p. 80.

[14] "The Patriarchal Family", *The Dynamics of World History*, p. 161.

[15] Ibid., pp. 161–62.

[16] *De Bono Conjugali* iii.3, PL 40, 375: "Quod mihi non videtur propter solam filiorum procreationem, sed propter ipsam etiam naturalem in diverso sexu societatem. Alioquin non jam diceretur conjugium in senibus, p[r]æsertim si vel amisissent filios, vel minime genuissent. Nunc vero in bono licet annoso conjugio, etsi emarcuit ardor ætatis inter masculum et feminam, viget tamen ordo charitatis inter maritum et uxorem. . . . Deinde quia reprimitur, et quodam modo verecundius æstuat concupiscentia carnis, quam temperat parentalis affectus. Intercedit enim quædam gravitas fervidæ voluptatis, cum in eo quod

sibi vir et mulier adhærescunt, pater et mater esse meditantur." See Peter Brown, *Augustine of Hippo* (Berkeley: University of California Press, 1967), p. 390.

[17] Ibid., xviii.21, PL 40, 387: "Sed quoniam ex multis animis una civitas futura est habentium animam unam et cor unum in Deum (Act. iv,32); quæ unitatis nostræ perfectio post hanc peregrinationem futura est, ubi omnium cogitationes nec latebunt invicem, nec inter se in aliquo repugnabunt: propterea Sacramentum nuptiarum temporis nostris sic ad unum virum et unam uxorem redactum est. . . ."

[18] Ibid., xxiv.32, PL 40, 394: "Bonum igitur nuptiarum per omnes gentes atque homines in causa generandi est, et in fide castitatis: quod autem ad populum Dei pertinet, etiam in sanctitate Sacramenti. . . ."

[19] See, for instance, Plato, *Phædrus*, 274–78; and Augustine, *Confessions*, IV, 10, XI, 3.

[20] *Christianity and the New Age* (1931; reprint, Manchester, N.H.: Sophia Institute Press, 1985), pp. 78–79.

[21] Ibid.

[22] *The Formation of Christendom*, p. 139.

[23] *Liturgy and Personality* (1960; reprint, Manchester, N.H.: Sophia Institute Press, 1986), p. 17.

[24] *Christianity and the New Age*, pp. 79–80.

[25] *Enarrationes in Psalmos* XXVI.ii.12, PL 36, 205: "Circumeat animus tuus per universam creaturam: undique tibi clamabit creatura: Deus me fecit."

[26] *In Omnes Psalmos Dilucida Explanatio* (Brixiæ, 1611), p. 124: "Igitur Propheta per contemplationem supra terrena omnia exaltatus, erumpit in admiratione operum Dei, & laudem opificis omnipotentis."

[27] *Progress and Religion* (1929; reprint, Garden City, N.Y.: Doubleday Image, 1960), p. 192.

[28] *Christianity and the New Age*, pp. 9–10.

[29] "How the World Lost Its Story", *First Things*, no. 36 (October 1993), pp. 19–24.

[30] *Progress and Religion*, p. 181.

[31] *Christianity and the New Age*, p. 103.

JAMES HITCHCOCK

# TO TEAR DOWN AND TO BUILD UP: CHRISTIANITY AND THE SUBVERSIVE FORCES IN WESTERN CIVILIZATION

Christianity was born when the Roman Empire was at its peak, and it is an appropriate paradox that, as the faith spread throughout the Empire, it helped both to subvert the long Roman hegemony and at the same time to preserve what was best in it. For Christopher Dawson, perhaps the most penetrating student of the relationship of religion and culture who has ever written, this paradox could be taken to sum up the entire role of the Church within history.

In many significant ways the Church simply replaced the Empire as the imperial structure fell away in the West. Bishops like Ambrose in Milan functioned as local leaders of a universal community which was now spiritual in nature rather than political but still offered men a sense of the ultimate unity of the human race.[1] The Church condemned what was sinful in the classical world, struggled to preserve what was valuable, and above all brought about a spiritual recovery which made a new synthesis of religion and culture possible.

In this as in so many other ways, Augustine of Hippo was a theologian whose influence could scarcely be exaggerated, including among other things nothing less than the first real Christian effort to see meaning in history, a discovery which freed Christians both from a nostalgic longing for a dead order and from an escape to a wholly mythical and atemporal world. As the Empire collapsed, the Church wed herself to the future of civilization and gladly accepted the burden of rebuilding.

History became the unfolding of the divine plan, governed by a universal order of reason, the beginning of the Kingdom of God which will never be adequately realized on earth. The Church now offered an alternative to the servile state, and she rendered moral freedom possible by depriving the State of its divine character while at the same time undergirding it with religious and moral purpose.

In *The Making of Europe*,[2] one of Dawson's best-known books, which has perhaps been more widely read than any of the others, he summarized the creative role of the Church in a sweeping way never before attempted by any other historian, showing in particular how the Church provided the West with a sense of unity which the Empire had provided only inadequately, including now a strong sense of spiritual purpose.

But this creative role was made possible only by the acceptance of martyrdom, and it was the martyrs' example above all which conveyed to mankind the spiritual power of the gospel, victory in defeat, strength in weakness. The Church was the only community within the Roman Empire which could not be absorbed by the all-encompassing State, even as she was impervious to the religious syncretism pervasive in the ancient world. The Church was not ultimately implicated in the fall of Rome, no matter how many catastrophes followed on that fall.

The monks, whose vocation was at one time thought of as a kind of bloodless martyrdom, became the most powerful spiritual leaders of the new age, confronting the barbarians—those brutal warriors who had directly subverted the Empire in the most ferocious way possible—with a power they could not fully comprehend but to which they ultimately bowed. St. Boniface in particular united Teutonic initiative and energy with the Roman sense of order, thus laying the foundations for what is now called the Middle Ages.

Although later generations tend to recall the "civilizing" mission of the monks of the Dark Ages, Dawson pointed out that they conceived their mission first of all in terms of judgment, pronouncing the power of God over sinners, and it was this spiritual toughness which made a new civilization possible. The monks themselves, having submitted to the hard discipline of their rule, could manifest to the world examples of viable human communities which were both free and regulated.[3]

The new synthesis which the Church produced from the ashes of the Empire was indeed long-lasting and, despite numerous crises during the Middle Ages, came to an end only with the Protestant Reformation, more than a millennium after Augustine had laid the foundations of Christendom.

The "subversion" by the Reformers was once again overt, involving as it did a direct assault on the spiritual authority of the Church and even a physical assault on the major manifestations of Christian civilization, such as churches and monasteries. Characteristically, Dawson concentrated not so much on formal doctrine as the chief issue of the sixteenth century but on such things as the destruction of religious art and above all the rejection of monasticism, the institution by which the Church had embodied her supernatural character in visible organized form.[4]

Noting that Martin Luther was a man of many books, running to many thousands of pages, while Ignatius Loyola was a man of only one, and that scarcely a book at all, Dawson pointed out how the incisive simplicity of the *Spiritual Exercises* exactly met the needs of the age for a new kind of Catholicism which was at the same time wholly orthodox. Ignatius began with a program for the spiritual revitalization of individuals, which in time became a program for the recovery of the entire Church.[5]

> Throughout there is little theology, and no intellectual discussion. It is a direct appeal to the will, based on one spiritual axiom, and to the imagination stimulated by the contemplation of the life of Christ. But this was sufficient to change men's lives and to bring about far-reaching changes in society and culture.[6]
>
> Above all there could be no question of their [the Jesuits'] orthodoxy. Yet he [Ignatius] was not precisely a reactionary or

a traditionalist. He had no prejudice against new methods or new ideas. Indeed he was the first to break with the age-old tradition of the community singing or recitation of the office by religious communities, and similarly all external rules and practices were reduced by him to a minimum. Everything was designed to make the Society of Jesus as flexible and united as possible, so that it would be free to turn its energies in whatever direction they were needed.[7]

But the ultimate recovery of the Church from the low point of the early sixteenth century was, in Dawson's view, the creation of Baroque culture, which reinvigorated the historic synthesis of classicism and Christianity, gave free rein to the human imagination in the service of God and countered Protestantism at precisely those points where it had attacked the Church most forcefully—its baptism of culture through the medium of the arts.[8]

> It was rather that the whole spirit of the culture was passionate and ecstatic, and finds its supreme expression in the art of music and in religious mysticism. . . . The bourgeois culture has the mechanical rhythm of a clock, the Baroque the musical rhythm of a fugue or sonata . . . the Baroque spirit lives in and for the triumphant moment of creative ecstasy. It will have all or nothing.[9]

The brilliant and devout Baroque culture was itself subverted rather quickly, notably by the French royal court, which tamed it and used it for political purposes. This later made possible the Enlightenment, an intellectual subversion of Christianity which in its turn directly prepared the way for the brutal frontal assault on the Church which was the French Revolution. By 1800, however, Western Christianity had lost most of its intellectual and artistic creativity, and it experienced a notable revival in the early nineteenth century mainly because of its survival among the common people, who were little affected by Enlightenment ideas and inclined if anything to be affronted by the excesses of the Revolution. Among them too the attractive power of martyrdom was formidable.[10]

The revival of religion which followed the French Revolution was not confined to any one country or to any single Church. It was common to the Latin and Germanic peoples and to Catholic and Protestant countries. Indeed it made itself felt far beyond the limits of organized Christianity and imparted a religious tendency to social and intellectual movements of the most diverse kinds, even though they were apparently in revolt against everything orthodox and traditional, either in the sphere of religion or of morals. Christianity . . . was brought back to the court and the salon, and even those who rejected it no longer did so in the contemptuous and cocksure manner of the man of the Enlightenment.

This revival of belief in religion, or at least a respect for religion, is the more remarkable when we contrast it with the external losses which religion had suffered during the preceding period. In sheer material destruction of monasteries and churches, in confiscation of property and abrogation of privileges, the Age of the Revolution far surpassed that of the Reformation; it was in fact a second Reformation, but a frankly anti-religious one.

Yet the very violence of the storm revealed the strength of those religious forces which the eighteenth century had ignored. The persecution itself did much to restore the prestige of religion and of the clergy by investing them with the halo of martyrdom. . . . Thus the Revolution, which was the child of the Enlightenment, also proved to be its destroyer.[11]

But the religious revival which occurred after the defeat of Napoleon also paved the way for perhaps the most seductive subversion which Christianity has yet experienced, a subversion whose process is still operative today, and one which many Christians cannot even recognize. Nineteenth-century liberalism in effect established a new creed, much of it based on the moral teachings of Christianity, even as social custom in the West came to support religion of some vague and bland kind, so that it was possible for the well-meaning individual to regard genuine Christianity as almost synonymous with enlightened citizenship, a temptation rendered all the more attractive by the material prosperity which capitalism created, which was itself ratified by the doctrine of progress, understood now in a wholly secular sense.[12]

Dawson began his intellectual career shortly after the First World War, and by then the collapse of this seductive liberalism had already become apparent. Faith in progress had eroded, and it was no longer possible to believe that science would of itself insure a better future. Liberal idealism was in retreat, having undermined the very moral foundations on which it rested. At the same time Dawson cautioned Christians not to rejoice in the decline of nineteenth-century humanitarianism, since the Church is not indifferent to the movement of history. Much that was good was being lost.[13]

> In reality Christianity creates the motive power—spiritual will —on which all true progress must ultimately rest. Without this spiritual foundation all progress in knowledge or wealth only extends the range of human suffering, and the possibilities of social disorder. All the great movements, which have built up modern secular civilization, have been more or less vitiated by this defect. . . . The only final escape for humanity from this heartbreaking circle of false starts and frustrated hopes is through the conquest of the world by charity—the coming of the Kingdom of God.[14]

The period between the world wars saw the rise of totalitarianisms of both the right and the left, and in some ways this dominated Dawson's formative years as a student of history. In his view such totalitarianism was virtually inevitable once a civilization had lost its soul.[15] Christianity was locked into a struggle with Marxism particularly, because both claimed to understand and to value history.[16]

But the obvious threats which the dictatorships posed to the Church were in some ways less dangerous than those of the democratic states, precisely because of the inconspicuousness of the latter. As early as the 1920s Dawson was beginning to see that even the liberal states were moving toward a kind of totalitarianism, which he defined not as dictatorship but as mass consciousness and mass organization. The most dangerous form of this subversion of Christian beliefs had been accepted even by many Christians because it was so taken for granted—the State's monopoly over education. The Church could endure persecution but could not surrender her right to teach, Dawson insisted. Yet the Church was being crushed by the universal welfare state which would absorb all the Church's secondary functions.[17]

One of Dawson's most brilliant insights into the nature of the problem was his 1930 analysis of what was later called the Sexual Revolution. The Church, he noted, had reestablished the family in the postclassical age but had placed it on a far more solid foundation than the Romans had done. In the nineteenth century, however, family life had been all but destroyed by the forces of industrialization. Sex itself had come to be glorified and had been severed from the idea of procreation. The result was an unthinking popular hedonism, a situation in which the State was able to control and dominate the family, which no longer had a firm sense of its own identity. Dawson, writing before the modern age of officially promoted contraception, even predicted accurately the way in which the older population strains in Europe and America would cease to reproduce themselves and would give way to migrant peoples.[18] In a memorable phrase at another time, Dawson contrasted two different kinds of totalitarianism—castor oil and concentration camps versus free milk and contraceptives.[19]

> The true way of spiritualizing sex is not to idealise our emotions and to hide physical appetite under a cloud of sentiment, but rather to bring our sexual life into relation with a more universal reality. The romantic idealization of passion and the rationalist attempt to reduce love to the satisfaction of physical desire, alike fail to create that permanent basis of sexual life which can only be found in a spiritual order which transcends the appetites and the self-will of the individual. It is only when a man accepts marriage as something greater than himself, a sacred obligation

to which he must conform himself, that he is able to realize all his spiritual and social possibilities.[20]

As in the waning days of the Roman Empire, the Church was in the paradoxical position, according to Dawson, of seeking to redeem the very society which was subverting her beliefs, and indeed the Church was the only force capable of bringing about such a redemption, through her universalism, her spirituality and her profound understanding of human nature.[21]

> Thus Christianity, more than any other religion, is characterized by its doctrine of spiritual renewal and regeneration. It stands for the restoration or transformation of human nature in Christ —in other words the creation of a new humanity. This great central truth has been obscured and often forgotten by the religious individualism of the last two or three centuries, which conceived salvation as a happy after-life to be attained by pious individuals as the reward of their moral perfection, or their religious practices. But the Christian idea of salvation is essentially social.[22]

At times Dawson believed that the future of Christianity in the West looked optimistic, noting for example the Catholic intellectual revival which seemed to show that the Church was "returning from the desert".[23] Communication between the Church and modern culture was not completely blocked, he thought, and the anti-religious movements might provoke an opposite reaction.[24] The City of God is always stronger than it looks, as the City of Man is weaker.[25] In the world after 1945 he detected a return to "corporate" ways of thinking, such as myth and ritual, which might be the basis for a genuine religious revival.[26]

But even in his optimistic moments, Dawson was sceptical of some of the obvious ways of rechristianizing culture. There could no longer be such a thing as a Catholic society, he thought, and religiously based political parties were also not a solution. Clerical politics was ill-advised, since historically prelates (Cardinals Wolsey and Richelieu, for example) had been among the worst betrayers of the Church's interests.[27] At the same time the modern Popes, especially Pius XII, had outlined a comprehensive theory of society based on the idea of a natural law binding on all peoples across cultural, political and even religious lines.[28]

Throughout most of his career, Dawson's view of the United States was negative, a logical deduction from his diagnosis of unfettered greed and unfettered technology as the causes of most of the problems of the modern world. By the 1950s, however, he had begun to notice signs of spiritual vitality in this country, based on its religious heritage and its tradition of religious freedom. Both those traditions had made American religion too individualistic and subjective, however, and American Catholics had failed to use their freedom in effective ways. But the United States remained a society of considerable promise, he finally concluded.[29]

He was led to that judgment partly by closer familiarity with American society, including a term teaching at Harvard University, but even more by his gradual estimate that the best practical solution to the spiritual crisis of the West was the systematic study of "Christian culture", a task at which even Catholic colleges and universities (most of which were in the United States) had not done well. Such an approach could put students in touch with their spiritual roots, and thus prepare them for a transforming role in society, and could even persuade nonbelievers to recognize that those roots were indeed Christian and had to be respected. This controversial proposal resulted in one of Dawson's best-known and enduring books, *The Crisis of Western Education*.

To survey today the great sweep of Western Christian history which Christopher Dawson did so much to illuminate is to reach the melancholy conclusion that virtually all the historical factors which served the cause of religion in the past are now absent. The religious orders which served as models of ordered communities in the Dark Ages are now themselves often models of demoralized disorder. There are few missionaries, and some of those have serious doubts about the legitimacy of their calling. Unlike the days of the Roman Empire, the State is not in decline but in fact moves precisely toward the kind of seductive totalitarianism which Dawson predicted. Political prelates remain as unreliable as ever. While there is no absence of Christian martyrs in various parts of the world, their existence seems often an embarrassment to Western Christians, who prefer to keep them out of sight. No great age of cultural creativity like that of the Baroque seems likely, and the masses of ordinary people, far from being repositories of an untroubled faith, are among the first victims of corrosive ideas spread through the mass media.

Yet Dawson, although he never tired of admonishing his fellow Christians to take history seriously and to realize that the Church seeks to transform culture, not to abandon it, also saw that the mystery of faith dictates that Christian fulfillment is often not discernible in history, and he also had words for a pessimistic time.

Even when he expressed belated admiration for American Catholicism, he pointed out that it had come into being almost entirely in the most recent period of Church history (post-1850), which had essentially been an age of defeat.[30] Indeed, much of Christian history has been lived as defeat, even as the early Christian offered the world "the Cross alone" but thereby called a new world into being.[31] Christians are pioneers of a new movement of world revolution, but its contours are hidden from them.[32] Totalitarianism can only be resisted on religious grounds, and Catholics alone are capable of getting in contact with their spiritual roots.[33] The modern Church is now in a situation like that of the early Church, although it is not at all certain that modern Christians are capable of the same spiritual heroism.[34]

> In these grim times it may seem unreal to speak of the prospects of a new Christian order. But if Christianity is not suited to hard times, Christians have no right to speak at all.[35]
> Christianity, on the other hand, offers no immediate panacea

for the complex malady of the modern world. It has eternity before it, and it can afford to take its time. But for that very reason a Christian culture is potentially wider and more catholic than a secular one. It is God-centered, not man-centered, and it consequently changes the whole pattern of human life by setting it in a new perspective.[36]

The paradox of historic Christianity was that Christians who were indifferent to worldly results often turned out to be the guardians and servants of human life.[37] Christianity makes a difference in the world ultimately because Christians have knowledge of the world to come, which alters the entire focus of their understanding, revealing the end of life itself.[38] Christian principles do not "work" in any empirical sense, and often Christians lack knowledge even of the strategies they must use for the future. Christianity is not social reform but light in a dark place.[39]

Thus at various times in his life Dawson thought that an apocalyptic stance was appropriate, warning that persecution lay ahead,[40] and, were he alive today, he would probably judge this to be such a time. The Church does not wait for solid foundations to be laid but sows her seeds broadcast, relying on the will of God in history.[41] Dawson's words at the beginning of World War II are if anything even more compelling fifty years later:

The Spirit blows through the world like wind and fire, driving the kingdoms before it, burning up the works of man like the dry grass, but the meaning of history is found not in the wind or the fire, but in the "small voice" of the Word which is never silent, . . . but which cannot bear fruit unless man cooperates by an act of faith and spiritual obedience. This dynamic and prophetic element is an essential part of the Christian tradition, and it is present even in periods when the Church seemed bound to a fixed and changeless order. . . .

Today Christianity is implicated in history just as much as Israel was in the age of the prophets . . . there is already a general realization that social and political issues have become spiritual issues—that the Church cannot abstain from intervention without betraying its mission . . . it is not due to the advance of the Christian element in our civilization and the reconquest of the world for God. Quite the contrary. It is due to the invasion of the spiritual by the temporal, the triumphant self-assertion of secular civilization and of the secular state against the Church.[42]

In the end even the greatest Catholic historian of culture could do no better than to remind us that history is always a tragedy and a failure whose meaning will be known only at the end of time,[43] that the world is always ending, each end a rehearsal for the final end.[44]

For though the Church no longer inspires and dominates the external culture of the modern world, it still remains guardian of all the riches of its own inner life and is the bearer of a sacred tradition. If society were once again to become Christian, after a generation or two or ten or twenty generations, this sacred tradition would once more flow out into the world and fertilize the culture of societies yet unborn. Thus the movement toward Christian culture is at one and the same time a voyage into the unknown, in the course of which new worlds of human experience will be discovered, and a return to our own fatherland—the sacred tradition of the Christian past which flows underneath the streets and cinemas and skyscrapers of the new Babylon as the tradition of the patriarchs and prophets flowed beneath the palaces and amphitheaters of Imperial Rome.[45]

# NOTES

[1] "St. Augustine and His Age", *Enquiries into Religion and Culture* (New York: Sheed & Ward, 1937), pp. 198–258.

[2] (New York: Sheed & Ward, 1932.)

[3] *Religion and the Rise of Western Culture* (New York: Sheed & Ward, 1950), pp. 29, 31, 33, 43, 51.

[4] *The Dividing of Christendom* (New York: Sheed & Ward, 1965), pp. 119–23.

[5] Ibid., pp. 124–25.

[6] Ibid., p. 125.

[7] Ibid., p. 128.

[8] Ibid., pp. 156–65; *Progress and Religion* (New York: Sheed & Ward, 1929), p. 144; "Catholicism and the Bourgeois Mind", *The Dynamics of World History*, ed. John J. Mulloy (LaSalle, Ill.: Sherwood Sugden, 1978), p. 207; *The Movement of World Revolution* (New York: Sheed & Ward, 1959), pp. 43–52.

[9] *The Dynamics of World History*, p. 207.

[10] *The Movement of World Revolution*, pp. 52, 66; *Progress and Religion*, p. 157; *Beyond Politics* (New York: Sheed & Ward, 1939), p. 71; *The Gods of Revolution* (London: Sidgwick & Jackson, 1972), pp. 129–45.

[11] *The Gods of Revolution*, pp. 129–30, 132.

[12] *Progress and Religion*, pp. 149, 154, 157; "The End of an Age", *The Criterion* 9 (April 1930), pp. 390, 396; "The New Decline and Fall", *The English Review* 53 (June-December 1931), p. 416; *Religion and the Modern State* (New York: Sheed & Ward, 1936), p. 133.

[13] *Progress and Religion*, pp. 172, 174, 178, 188, 193, 263; "General Introduction" to *Essays in Order* (New York: Macmillan Co., 1931), vols. 1–3, pp. v, viii, xi; "The End of an Age", pp. 386, 390; "The Nature and Destiny of Man", *Enquiries into Religion and Culture*, p. 343; *Religion and the Modern State*, p. 64. "Hope and Culture", *Lumen Vitæ* 9:3 (July-September 1954), pp. 427, 429.

[14] *Enquiries into Religion and Culture*, p. 343.

[15] "The New Decline and Fall", pp. 413, 421; "The End of an Age", p. 399; *Religion and the Modern State*, pp. 1, 8, 44; "Civilization in Crisis", *The Catholic World*, 182:1070 (January 1956), p. 248.

[16] *Religion and the Modern State*, pp. 59, 73–84.

[17] Ibid., pp. 55, 57, 105–9, 113; *Beyond Politics*, pp. 28, 68, 78, 92; "Religious Liberty and the New Political Forces", *The Month*, 183:955 (January 1947), pp. 41–44; *Understanding Europe* (New York: Sheed & Ward, 1952), p. 241; "The European Revolution", *The Catholic World*, 179:1070 (May 1954),

p. 88; "Civilization in Crisis", pp. 251–52; "The Challenge of Secularism", *The Catholic World*, 182:1091 (February 1956), p. 326; *The Movement of World Revolution*, pp. 77–78.

[18] "Christianity and Sex", *Enquiries into Religion and Culture*, pp. 259–91.

[19] *Religion and the Modern State*, p. 108.

[20] *Enquiries into Religion and Culture*, p. 290.

[21] "The New Leviathan", Ibid., p. 17; "General Introduction" to *Essays in Order*, pp. xvi, xx; "The End of an Age", p. 399; *Religion and the Modern State*, pp. 97, 103, 111, 138, 140; *Beyond Politics*, pp. 21, 23, 88; *The Judgement of the Nations* (New York: Sheed & Ward, 1942), pp. 130, 144; *Understanding Europe*, pp. 221, 227; "Spiritual Reconstruction: The Roman Catholic View", *The Future of Faith*, ed. Percy Carlson (London: Hurst & Blackwell, 1942), p. 70.

[22] *The Judgement of the Nations*, pp. 130–31.

[23] "General Introduction" to *Essays in Order*, p. xvi.

[24] *The Modern Dilemma* (New York: Sheed & Ward, 1933), pp. 99, 106; "Religion and Life", *Enquiries into Religion and Culture*, p. 299.

[25] *Religion and the Modern State*, p. 152.

[26] *The Movement of World Revolution*, p. 79.

[27] *The Judgement of the Nations*, pp. 119, 206; *The Historic Reality of Christian Culture* (New York: Sheed & Ward, 1960), p. 42; *Religion and the Modern State*, p. 122.

[28] *Religion and the Modern State*, p. 130; *The Judgement of the Nations*, p. 164; "Foundations of European Order", *The Catholic Mind*, 42:977 (May 1944), p. 315; "Christian Unity and the New Order", *The Sword of the Spirit*, 13 (January 18, 1941), p. 2; "Restoration of Natural Law", ibid., 93 (May 1946), p. 2; "Spiritual Reconstruction", p. 1.

[29] "Christianity and Sex", p. 259; "Religious Liberty and the New Political Forces", p. 45; "Catholics in the Modern World", *The Tablet*, 195:5740 (May 27, 1950), p. 419; "Dealing with the Enlightenment and Liberal Ideology", *The Commonweal*, 60:6 (May 14, 1954), p. 138; *America and the Secularization of Modern Culture* (Houston: University of St. Thomas, 1960), pp. 16, 17, 22; "American Education and Christian Culture", *American Benedictine Review*, 9:1–2 (Spring-Summer 1958), p. 267; *The Crisis of Western Education* (New York: Sheed & Ward, 1961), pp. 109–11.

[30] *The Historic Reality of Christian Culture*, p. 57.

[31] *Religion and the Modern State*, p. 119.

[32] Ibid., p. 153.

[33] "Europe and Christendom", *The Dublin Review*, 209:419 (October 1941), p. 118; *The Judgement of the Nations*, p. 184; "Christian Unity and the New Order", p. 10.

[34] "Religious Liberty and the New Political Forces", p. 41; "Hope and Culture", p. 430; "The Future of Christian Culture", *The Commonweal*, 59:24

(March 19, 1954), p. 598; *The Historic Reality of Christian Culture*, p. 85; *The Crisis of Western Education*, p. 179.

[35] *The Judgement of the Nations*, p. 184.

[36] *The Crisis of Western Education*, p. 179.

[37] *The Historic Reality of Christian Culture*, p. 66.

[38] *Religion and the Modern State*, pp. 123, 125.

[39] "The Tragedy of Christian Politics", *The Sign*, 18:1 (August 1938), p. 8; *Beyond Politics*, p. 88; "The Christian View of History", *The Dynamics of World History*, pp. 237, 247, 250; *The Historic Reality of Christian Culture*, p. 25.

[40] "The Outlook for Christian Culture Today", *Cross Currents*, 5:2 (Spring 1955), pp. 132-33, 135-36; *The Movement of World Revolution*, p. 102; *The Historic Reality of Christian Culture*, p. 25.

[41] "The Remaking of Europe", *The Tablet*, 168:5004 (April 4, 1936), p. 146; "The Hour of Darkness", ibid., 174:5195 (December 2, 1939), p. 625; "The Kingdom of God in History", *The Dynamics of World History*, pp. 270, 286.

[42] *The Judgement of the Nations*, pp. 152-53.

[43] "Kingdom of God in History", p. 286.

[44] "The Tragedy of Christian Politics", p. 10.

[45] *The Historic Reality of Christian Culture*, pp. 29-30.

RUSSELL HITTINGER

# CHRISTOPHER DAWSON ON
# TECHNOLOGY AND THE
# DEMISE OF LIBERALISM

I

Having accepted the Stillman Chair of Catholic Studies at
Harvard, Christopher Dawson arrived in New York City on
September 30, 1958. He summarized his impression of the new
world in this way:

> No one from the Old World can land at New York without be-
> ing immediately impressed by this spectacle of gigantic material
> power. . . . There is nothing like it in Europe or I think any-
> where else. It seems to mark the coming of a new age and a new
> civilization. . . . But viewed in the perspective of history it is a
> very strange and surprising thing. The ancient Egyptians built
> pyramids that were even greater than the skyscrapers of New
> York, in terms of the human effort expended, but they were
> for the tombs of God-Kings. The relatively poverty stricken
> peoples of medieval Europe erected vast cathedrals and abbeys,
> but these were the expression of their common faith and their
> hopes for eternity. But to-day we build temples greater than the
> Egyptian pyramids or the Gothic Cathedrals and they are ded-
> icated to toothpaste or chewing gum or anything that anyone
> wants. . . ."[1]

One might suspect that these were the grumpy remarks of an
Englishman who was born in 1899, in a twelfth-century Welsh
castle. But Dawson was only preparing his audience for a far
more serious evaluation of the culture. Modern technology,
he went on to say, is a "Frankenstein" that increases govern-

73

mental power and decreases individual liberty.[2] Of course, this
was a time in which Americans thought rather well of themselves. But Dawson contended that the ideology of the Cold
War distracts our attention from the fact that the democracies
and the totalitarian regimes converge in at least one important respect: namely, that they are planned societies, organized
around technology, and governed by technocratic elites.[3] Dawson concluded by insisting that "the ultimate issue for modern civilization" is the recovery of a humanism sufficient to
withstand "the disintegrating and dehumanizing influences of
technology".[4]

It would be a mistake to attribute Dawson's remarks about
technology to his aristocratic dislike of Gotham and to his even
deeper antipathy for the managerial class. I say that it would be
a mistake, because such remarks were not mere *obiter dicta*. In
fact, Dawson's criticism of the technological society is one of
the most persistent themes in his books and lectures. From his
first published work, *Progress and Religion* (1929), to the lectures given during the twilight of his career in America, he was
emphatic in the judgment that the chief enemy of culture is not
liberalism or the other secular religions of progress but technology. The secular religions of progress which arose during
the eighteenth and nineteenth centuries expressed an older humanistic culture, going back at least to the Renaissance. These
ideologies defined progress in humane terms. They envisioned
perfections which belong or ought to belong to individuals:
for example, enlightenment, benevolence, justice and rights.
In Dawson's estimation, however, liberalism was a transitory
and relatively brief phase of culture, lasting less than a century.
It was a mere bit player on a stage controlled by larger forces,
which measured progress in terms of an array of tools, not the
least of which are the methods of the managerial class. This
class that represented to Dawson what St. Paul meant when
he spoke of the "Cosmocrats of the Dark Æon"—that is, of
rational powers which make use of things below reason to conquer and rule the world of man.

I must admit that in previous readings of Dawson's work, I was not persuaded by the critical, if not apocalyptic, remarks he made about technology. But the thesis that technology is the basis of secular culture, and that liberalism was but a transitory phrase en route to technocracy, was argued so forcefully, from the beginning to the end of his career, that we ought to take stock of what he had to say.

This afternoon I will revisit Dawson's thought on this subject. First, I will give a Dawsonian definition of liberalism. In particular, I want to mention why Dawson thought that liberalism was a humane culture, and why we should fear, rather than gloat over, its demise. Second, I will discuss his thesis that technology is the real basis of secular culture, that liberalism failed to control technology, by failing to assign to the machine some end beyond a merely materialistic idea of progress and well-being. Third, I will take one technology as a case in point illustrating Dawson's thesis.

## II

Rush Limbaugh notwithstanding, there is no precise definition of liberalism, either in ordinary speech or in professional scholarship. Liberalism can denote institutions and cultural practices, as well as ideas and theories about those institutions and practices. In the nineteenth century, especially in the Anglophone world, liberalism first denoted a set of ideas about how the legal system ought to be reformed, particularly the system of criminal law. Liberals like Jeremy Bentham and John Stuart Mill argued that the penal code should reflect enlightened principles of social utility rather than the moral taboos and passions of public opinion. Reform of the penal system was the pivotal idea for a broad-ranging set of reforms concerning child labor, mandatory education, women's suffrage and economic markets. In all of these areas, and in many more, the liberal called first for legal and then for full-scaled institutional reforms which separated the coercive force of law from the customary notions of morality. The liberal believed that the individual, emancipated from the public force of religion and custom, is the engine of cultural, economic and even religious creativity. (No doubt Pope Pius IX had all of this in mind when he declared in 1854 that it is "an error to believe that the Roman pontiff can or should reconcile himself to, and agree with progress, liberalism and modern civilizations".)[5]

It would be impossible to give a definition that captures (at a proper level of detail and complexity) all of the different aspects and phases of liberalism. Rather than define it, I will read a single passage from J. S. Mill's *On Liberty* (1859). If this text does not capture the soul of liberalism, then I suspect that nothing will. Mill wrote that:

> There is always need of persons not only to discover new truths and point out when what were once truths are true no longer, but also to commence new practices and set the example of more enlightened conduct and better taste and sense in human life. This cannot well be gainsaid by anybody who does not believe that the world has already attained perfection in all its ways and practices. It is true that this benefit is not capable of being rendered by everybody alike; there are but few persons, in comparison with the whole of mankind, whose experiments, if adopted by others, would be likely to be any improvement on established practice. But these few are the salt of the earth; without them, human life would become a stagnant pool. Not only is it they who introduce good things which did not before exist; it is they who keep the life in those which already exist. . . .There is only too great a tendency in the best beliefs and practices to degenerate into the mechanical; and unless there were a succession of persons whose ever-recurring originality prevents the grounds of those beliefs and practices from becoming merely traditional . . . there would be no reason why civilization should not die out. . . .[6]

Mill went on to add the following thought:

> The progressive principle . . . whether as the love of liberty or of improvement, is antagonistic to the sway of custom, in-

volving at least emancipation from that yoke; and the contest between the two constitutes the chief interest of the history of mankind. . . .[7] Europe is, in my judgment, wholly indebted to this plurality of paths for its progressive and many-sided development.[8]

This, I propose, is the genuine article. Liberalism was not a theory of democracy. Liberals of all stripes, from Mill to de Tocqueville, feared the leveling effects of democracy, egalitarianism and mass public opinion. Nor should liberalism be equated with the rationalism of the Enlightenment, for liberals championed the spontaneous genius, who more resembled the artist than the scientist or the philosopher. In this regard, it should be recalled that liberalism arose during the period of Romanticism. Nor should liberalism be equated with the scientific rationality of the industrial revolution, for liberals also feared the alliance between democratic opinion and the machine. Indeed, in *On Liberty* the machine is almost always the metaphor for the anti-liberal principle.

The idea of the free market of economic exchange was actually a small piece of a much larger metaphor of the free market of ideas, of what Mill called "experiments in living". For the liberal, the State and its rule of law had the limited role of providing only the skeletal structure of procedures which facilitate the liberty of individuals. Liberals contended that the State should not have the role of central planning or management. Adam Smith, for example, observed that the legislator "seems to imagine that he can arrange the different members of a great society with as much ease as the hand arranges the different pieces upon a chessboard. He does not consider that . . . in the great chessboard of human society, every single piece has a principle of motion of its own. . . ."[9] It was a chief tenet of the liberal creed that society must defer to this individual "principle of motion". The liberal believed that any social order worth living in will emerge in unplanned ways, as a result of individual creativity.

Of course, liberals devoted themselves to a plethora of reform movements which used coercive power to change the law; but, at least in theory, these reforms were not supposed to dictate, from on high, the results of individual liberty; rather, they were meant to remove cultural and societal impediments to liberty.

Liberalism was truly a new and awesome idea of how culture ought to be reproduced. It was to be reproduced, not by custom and habit, not by central management, but pell-mell, by spontaneous individual choices. For the liberal, individual liberty is the goose that lays the golden egg. Of course, liberalism never was purely embodied in any nation or political party—and history clearly teaches the liberals could not resist using governmental power to make the goose lay the egg. But here, we are speaking of liberalism as an ideal; and, as an ideal that captured the imagination of the educated classes of the West, it was different from other secular religions of progress (for example, Marxism) precisely because it eschewed the idea that progress is dependent on the coercive apparatus of Caesar.

## III

Dawson was very respectful of liberalism. In a number of his books, he depicted it as a secularized version of Augustine's doctrine of the two cities. In the *City of God*, St. Augustine depicts two cities. On the one hand, there is the *civitas terrena*, which because of self-love is always dying and therefore cannot be an agent of progress. At best, the earthly city can maintain a kind of external order of justice. On the other hand, there is the *civitas Dei*, temporally embodied in the Church. This city, bound together by charity rather than coercion, is the agent of progress. As Dawson writes, Augustine's theology deprived "the state of its aura of divinity", and "for all its unworldliness, first made possible the ideal of a social order resting on the free personality".[10]

Again, to quote Dawson:

It is only in Western Europe that the whole pattern of culture is to be found in a continuous succession and alternation of free spiritual movements; so that every century of Western history shows a change in the balance of cultural elements, and the appearance of some new spiritual force which creates new ideas and institutions and produces a further movement of social change.[11]

Of course, this sounds very similar to the passage we read earlier from Mill's *On Liberty*.[12] The liberal vision of history and culture, Dawson explained, took over from Christendom not only its universalism, its sense of a spiritual purpose higher than the State, but also its dualism—although now it is the Church that is "the liberal equivalent of the powers of darkness, while the children of this world have become the children of light".[13] Dawson called liberalism a "sublimated Christianity"[14]—a humanitarian Christianity, relieved of the burdens of the supernatural and ecclesial authority. But he argued that liberalism was not relieved of the archetypal pattern of Western culture; it only changed the dramatic cast of the story.

It should be emphasized that Dawson did not begrudge liberalism its virtues.

—It advocated limited government and taught that nothing of lasting value can take place behind the back of the moral effort of the free individual.[15]

—Despite its more or less explicit doctrine of individualism, liberal culture embodied a kind of humanitarian idealism.[16] Cruel penal codes were reformed, famine and disease were combated, education was mandated.[17]

—And despite its doctrine of emancipation from custom, in the golden age of liberalism (Victorian England and America at the turn of the century), the family thrived as an independent social unit. Though sentimentalized and privatized, the family was at least somewhat protected from the forces of government and the market.[18]

—It developed a system of economic markets, which Dawson said was a "vast cooperative effort" requiring "a very high degree of social discipline and organization".[19]

—Moreover, like the older pattern of Christendom, liberal culture was transnational, transethnic and transracial. Like the Christian missionaries of the sixteenth and seventeenth centuries, who took the religious seed of European culture to all the continents, liberalism also had international aspirations. The domestic reforms of liberal culture were exported internationally.

Thus, Dawson dreaded the passing of liberal culture, for its demise deprived the West of a cultural pattern that had persisted for nearly two millennia. In *The Judgement of the Nations*, he wrote that "Christians have no reason to look on the defeat of this spirit with complacency or indifference . . . [for] these [liberal] ideas are not empty abstractions. They are the foundations of human life; and when they are undermined, the whole edifice of civilization is dissolved. . . ."[20]

## IV

According to Dawson, liberalism was "transitional and impermanent", lasting for less than a century.[21] What took its place was what Dawson called "the planned society",[22] which aspires to reproduce culture by means of technology. Technological order, he claimed, is "now the real basis of secular culture."[23] The only thing it shares with liberalism is the faith in a progress that is merely temporal and this-worldly. In all of the other relevant respects, the new order is the opposite of liberalism. Where liberals had faith in individual liberty and creativity, the technological order bespeaks necessity and uniformity; where liberals wanted to break the monopoly of the State, the technological order guarantees that only the State can mobilize the forces necessary for basic human undertakings. But the most important point is that liberal culture was still humanistic; despite liberal ideas, most people continued to live in the fashion of what C. S. Lewis called "old Western man". Real secularism, according to Dawson, could not emerge until technology made it possible for most people to live without the ideals and practices of the older Western order. Modern science changed the way that the educated class conceived of the world; but technology changed the way people lived.

Now, it must be said that by technology Dawson did not mean science, which is simply the effort to understand the natural environment. Nor did he mean merely the tools of applied science, for example, steam engines, computers, and so on. Rather, he meant the systematic application of tools to culture, especially to those areas of culture that had always been reproduced by humanistic activity, for example, sexual intercourse, family, religion and economic exchange. In short, by technology, Dawson meant the practice(s), via an interlocking set of technologies, of treating culture in the same way that the tool treats the natural environment. And this is simply another way of saying that the tool is no longer an instrument but rather the measure of the humane world.

Modern technologies are not only "labor-saving" devices. A labor-saving device, like an automated farm implement or a piston, replaces repetitive human acts. But most distinctive of contemporary technology is the replacement of the human act, or of what the scholastic philosophers called the *actus humanus*. The machine reorganizes and to some extent supplants the world of human action, in the moral sense of the term.[24] Hence, the policy of mutual assured destruction supplants diplomacy; the contraceptive pill supplants chastity; the cinema supplants recreation, especially prayer; managerial and propaganda techniques replace older practices and virtues of loyalty, and so on. Therefore, it is important to understand that Dawson's criticism of technology is not aimed at the tool per se. His criticism has nothing to do with the older and, in our context, misleading notion of "labor-saving" devices. Rather, it is aimed at a new cultural pattern in which tools are either deliberately designed to replace the human act or at least have the unintended effect of making the human act unnecessary or subordinate to the machine. Of course, Dawson did not live to see the emergence of "virtual-reality" technology, but he would have recognized it as part (perhaps the culminating part) of the continuum of technologies that he had in mind.

Consider, for example, the following remark written in 1870 by a British officer in the Indian Civil Service:

> Railways are opening the eyes of the people who are within reach of them. . . . They teach them that time is worth money, and induce them to economise that which they had been in the habit of slighting and wasting; they teach them that speed attained is time, and therefore money, saved or made. . . . Above all, they induce in them habits of self-dependence, causing them to act for themselves promptly and not lean on others.[25]

What is most striking about this statement is that the machine is regarded as the proximate cause of the liberal virtues; habits of self-dependence are the effect of the application of a technology. The benighted peoples of the subcontinent are to be civilized, not by reading Cicero, not by conversion to the Church of England, not even by adopting the liberal faith, but by receiving the discipline of trains and clocks. The machine is both the exemplar and the proximate cause of individual and cultural perfection.

The quote is also interesting because it supports Dawson's notion that liberalism was unable to impart liberal culture to non-Western peoples. (I cannot think of a single non-Western culture that was liberalized in the nineteenth or twentieth century.) Rather, the liberal imparted to these peoples Western technology: principally, military and managerial techniques, as well as the technologies of mass culture, especially those related to the entertainment industry and to propaganda.

It is worth mentioning that John Dewey's most popular book, *Reconstruction in Philosophy* (1920), was based upon his lectures in Tokyo, Peking and Nanking. Dewey preached abroad what he preached at home: namely, that the main purpose of the human mind is not truth but praxis; we think not so much to know but to change our environment, especially the human environment. Above all, Dewey taught that we must have the audacity to think and to act beyond the limits of traditional habits and customs. Yet, as Americans discovered in 1941, the Japanese did not become liberals; rather, they became armed to the teeth. And even after we imposed a liberal constitution on Japan after the War, it was a mere legal template laid over a modern technological society. In fact, postwar Japan was the first industrial society to sponsor abortion and contraception. Dawson believed that liberalism weakened the immune systems of traditional cultures; and indeed history itself testifies to the fact that rather than moving from Confucianism to liberalism, they moved straightaway to the ideal of the social engineer. They became modernized and adopted the economic, social and military imperatives of the machine.

Today, across all of the different political cultures, technology is required for the State's administration, for its military security, its propaganda, its markets, indeed for its very legitimacy. Governments rise and fall on the basis of their success in supplying the population with the technological means to achieve temporal happiness. The older liberal ideals of limited government, individual creativity, of an autonomous private sphere more or less immune from centralized planning are violated whenever the technological imperative dictates otherwise.

In this respect, liberalism everywhere failed to hold the line. It did not control the erosion of local liberty by nation states, but rather on its cultural watch the individual became dependent on government in ways that would have been unimaginable by despots of the old regime; local liberty became nothing more than a euphemism for a different sector of the nation state's administration. It did not check the ideology of planned economies; rather, in what may be the cruelest irony of all for the liberal, the term liberalism became synonymous with the State-managed economy; in all of the Western democracies today, the "liberal" party stands for a State-managed economy. It did not succeed in its cultural mission of creating societies based upon freedom and persuasion but rather succumbed to the militarization of State and to the creation of new police powers and systems of surveillance.

Dawson held that liberal culture paved the way for the technological order by separating the private and the public spheres, leaving the latter defenseless against the new technologies.[26] It was the ideal, and, to some extent, the practice, of liberalism to prohibit the State from acting for substantive moral and religious ends. The public sector was enlisted to facilitate what seemed, at first, to be relatively noncontroversial, even "neutral" ends: for example, security from enemies abroad and material well-being at home. These ends do not seem to dictate to the individual any particular version of the good life. Left to his own private discretion, the individual seemed to remain his own "principle of motion".

It is easy to understand why the liberal would regard technological order as something that leaves liberal values intact. Technology is not an ideology or a religion; it is not a person or even an institution. Nor does it have any inherent cultural properties; for we see that technology can be transferred from culture to culture, working just as well in Cambodia as in Cleveland. But, of course, modern technology is not neutral. In *The Judgement of the Nations*, Dawson explained that

> the spiritual elements in the Liberal culture were not strong enough to control the immense forces which had been released by the progress of the applied sciences and the new economic techniques. The advent of the machine, which was in a sense the result of the liberal culture, proved fatal to the liberal values and ideals, and ultimately to the social types which had been the creators and bearers of the culture.[27]

The new technological order exacted as its first price the liberal, who it made obsolete (the Hillary Clintons of this world only pronounce a humanitarian benediction over the work of the social engineer); but the technological order exacted as its ultimate price the traditional humanistic culture, of which the liberal was bearer. By 1942, Dawson concluded that this transition was complete and, for any foreseeable future, irreversible.

## V

There are a myriad of examples which could be cited to illustrate why this conviction about the neutrality of technology is mistaken. But I will give one specific example, which happens to be one that Dawson himself discussed in an essay entitled "The Patriarchal Family in History" (1933): namely, the problem of contraception. I will focus on contraception for three reasons: (1) Quite apart from any issues of moral theology (and I have no intention here of engaging in any moral homiletics on the subject), contraception is a civilizational issue because it bears upon the basic cell of society, the family; (2) contraception provides an especially vivid example of how a technology can completely reorganize a cultural order, from its system of justice, to its economic markets, to its religious institutions; (3) it is a case in point for how liberalism does not define or control but only rationalizes technology; by rationalize, I mean that liberal rhetoric only hands out permission slips, as it were, for bringing the individual under the dominion of technology.

Contraception has a long history, which I cannot rehearse in detail here. But I will pick the story up during the golden age of liberalism, which in this country would be the late nineteenth century. In the last decade of that century, the Massachusetts legislature passed an anti-contraceptive statute, which read, in part, as follows:

> Whoever sells, lends, gives away an instrument or other article intended to be used for self-abuse, or any drug, medicine, instrument or article whatever for the prevention of conception or for causing unlawful abortion, or advertises the same, or writes,

prints, or causes to be written or printed a card, circular, book, pamphlet, advertisement or notice of any kind stating when, where, how, of whom or by what means such articles can be purchased, obtained, or manufactured or makes any such article shall be punished. . . (Mass. c. 272, §21).

In 1917, this statute was interpreted by the Massachusetts Supreme Court in *Commonwealth v. Allison* (1917):

[Its] plain purpose is to protect purity, to preserve chastity, to encourage continence and self restraint, to defend the sanctity of the home, and thus to engender in the State and nation a virile and virtuous race of men and women.

Such statutes were passed by several state legislatures, consisting for the most part of secularized Protestants. Anti-contraceptive laws were but one facet of a larger reform movement that tried to protect the family, and women in particular, from the disintegrating forces of industrialization and the mass market. For example, laws were passed which held industry to higher standards with respect to female employees—precisely because they were mothers or prospective mothers. The Mann Act (1910) made it a felony to transport or to aid the transport of a woman in interstate commerce for the purpose of "debauchery".

The point I want to make is that even during the heyday of laissez-faire, the principle was well established, and often followed, that technology ought to be subordinated to society's moral interest in the family. With respect to contraceptives, it was a matter of common sense that, if widely distributed, they would undermine the principal cell of society. Writing in 1933, Dawson did not find it necessary to invoke any specifically Christian, much less Catholic, principles when he said that contraception "must lead inevitably to a social decadence far more rapid and more universal than that which brought about the disintegration of ancient civilization".[28] The patriarchal family, he noted:

requires chastity and self-sacrifice on the part of the wife and obedience and discipline on the part of the children, while even the father himself has to assume a heavy burden of responsibility and submit his personal feelings to the interests of the family . . . for these very reasons the patriarchal family is a much more efficient organ of cultural life. It is no longer limited to its primary sexual and reproductive functions. It becomes the dynamic principle of society and the source of social continuity.[29]

In 1930, Anglicans broke ranks with nearly the whole of Christian tradition with a declaration at the Lambeth Conference that permitted use of contraceptives by married couples, for grave reasons. Though the Anglicans greatly weakened the moral case against contraceptives, the Lambeth statement was exceedingly "conservative" and cautious by our standards today. The fact remained that, until the 1960s, no one claimed fundamental rights to have contraceptive sex; nor did anyone seriously challenge the authority of the State to pass morals legislation of this sort.

What changed? Was society more liberal in the 1960s than it was at the turn of the century? The change took place primarily because of a technological advance. The progesterone pill was developed in the late 1950s and shortly thereafter was marketed in the United States. The technological characteristic of the pill was crucial: orally administered, requiring no surgical procedure, it was seemingly a pill alongside other pills. Significantly, it was marketed as a birth-control pill rather than as a contraceptive. In a technological society, the word "control" signifies a responsible act. And because it was not a barrier method, even Catholic physicians argued that the pill was not a contraceptive.

Although barrier methods of contraception had been known about for decades, it was only after the introduction of the progesterone pill that there was any significant movement for a reform of the law. In 1965, in *Griswold v. Connecticut*, the Court found anti-contraceptive laws to be unconstitutional. In fact, the Court went so far as to invent a new, fundamental right of privacy. But what was especially interesting about the case is that, although this new right was justified in the name of individual liberty and marital privacy, it actually emancipated manufacturers and physicians. The Connecticut statute had not only prohibited the use of contraceptives, but had made criminally liable "[a]ny person who assists, abets, counsels, causes, hires or commands another to [use contraceptives]. . . ." The litigant in the case was not a married couple, suing over governmental intrusion into the sacred precincts of the bedroom; rather, the appellant, Dr. Buxton, was a professor at the Yale Medical School, who also served as Medical Director for Planned Parenthood. In other words, the rhetoric of individual liberty was mere window-dressing for a liberty of the manufacturers and purveyors of the pill, who allied themselves with the managerial class. This became undeniably clear in a 1977 case, *Carey v. Population Services*, when the state of New York's ban on the distribution of contraceptives to minors was challenged and found unconstitutional. Here, the Court said that "[r]estrictions on the distribution of contraceptives clearly burden[s] the freedom to make such [reproductive] decisions." Thus, what began rhetorically as a solemn right of married couples against the State became in reality a right of social engineers to accustom minors to the new standards of technological hygiene.

In *Roe v. Wade*, of course, the Court extended the right of privacy to abortion. Once again, it is interesting that the Court used the rhetoric of individual liberty to make more palatable a decision addressed chiefly to the technological elites, which in this case were medical professionals. Before writing his opinion, Justice Blackmun visited the Mayo Clinic, where he learned that anti-abortion legislation only had the goal of protecting women from incompetent medical procedures. Thus, the emergence of safe abortion procedures removed the rationale of those laws. The moral and legal orders, in other words, are to be defined by the efficiency of modern medicine. Indeed, the trimester scheme, which defined legal personhood in

terms of "viability", did not really designate ontological properties of the fetus so much as to align fetal development with
a medical schedule. (It is tantamount to the idea that someone
riding on Metro-North is a traveller, not by dint of being on
the train, but by virtue of whether he gets off at Pelham or
New Rochelle.)

In *Roe*, Justice Blackmun spoke in almost sacred terms, not
of the woman's liberty, but of her relationship to the physician. But even more to the point was the companion case, *Doe
v. Bolton* (1973), which effectively secured a right to abortion
on demand by defining the idea of maternal health so broadly
as to justify virtually all third-trimester abortions. In the *Doe*
case, the Court struck down any criteria other than the individual physician's "best clinical judgment" as the standard
for undertaking the abortion procedure. *Roe* and *Doe* did not
directly emancipate women but emancipated their physicians
—first from the police powers of the state governments and
then from their own hospitals and peer-review boards. In the
name of individual liberty, the multi-million-dollar industry of
the clinic was brought into being.

Twenty years later, in *Planned Parenthood v. Casey* (1992), the
Court reconsidered the constitutionality of *Roe*. Admitting that
the decision had dubious constitutional credentials, the Court
was remarkably candid about why it cannot be overturned:

> Abortion is customarily chosen as an unplanned response to
> the consequence of unplanned activity or to the failure of con-
> ventional birth control. . . . For two decades of economic and
> social developments, people have organized their intimate rela-
> tionships and made choices that define their views of themselves
> and their places in society, in reliance on the availability of abor-
> tion in the event that contraception should fail. The ability of
> women to participate equally in the economic and social life of
> the Nation has been facilitated by their ability to control their
> reproductive lives.

The key is the word "unplanned", for it indicates that human
activity is to be regarded in the same fashion as impersonal

nature. Like lightning, floods and tumors, the event of preg-
nancy follows a line of causality independent of a truly human
act; hence, it needs to be brought under the control of a technology. The Court frankly admitted not only that abortion is
practiced for the most part as ex post facto birth control but
that the practice has become a necessity.

In other words, the increments of legal emancipation track
the increments of technology, and the increments of technology are recast as kinds of social necessity. In order to make
room for what was, in itself, a relatively small part of the phar-
macological revolution, the entire legal and moral order of the
polity was changed: (1) the Bill of Rights was reinterpreted,
to make what was once homicide at criminal law a fundamental right at Constitutional law; (2) all common law pertain-
ing to the responsibility of husbands over wives and children
was summarily struck down; (3) divorce laws were changed;
(4) professional associations of physicians and lawyers changed
their by-laws to condemn any opposition to this continuum
of technologies; (5) churches changed their moral theologies
to accommodate the separation of sex and procreation; (6)
public school curricula changed, and indeed new cabinet of-
fices invented for the purpose of habituating even prepubescent
children to the use of the technology; (7) even a conservative
writer like George Will, who authored the book *Statescraft as
Soulcraft*, now recommends Norplant patches as a remedy for
the breakdown of the family in the inner city.

No culture would permit its basic institutions and practices
to be so dramatically changed simply by the dictate of individual liberty or, for that matter, as a rationalization for sexual
pleasure; the remarkably rapid nature of these changes can be
understood only if we realize that the technological order is
regarded as a necessity. And, as the ancient legal dictum put it,
"necessity knows no law".

I am not so naïve as to suggest that this one little device, swallowed with a glass of water, is the efficient cause of all of these troubles. The pill was received in the post-WWII suburbs, in which an array of technologies (chiefly the automobile) made possible a form of family life functionally independent of paternal authority. But the pill does give an especially vivid example of how the humane elements of a culture are reinterpreted to render technology immune from the direction of any higher principle. Even justice turns out to be the right of individuals to have equal access to the technology. The separation of sex from procreation, and the separation of procreation from the social roles and social virtues of motherhood, are not the result of feminism; rather, feminism is the result of these increments of technology. (The same can be said for homosexual parents. It is not merely coincidental that cultural and legal approbation of the homosexualist family followed after the contraceptive pill, and after the development of the in-vitro technologies which reproduce human life independent of any particular social form.)

Edmund Burke wrote that:

> To complain of the age we live in, to murmur at the present possessors of power, to lament the past, to conceive extravagant hopes of the future, are the common dispositions of the greatest part of mankind. . . . Such complaints and humours have existed in all times; yet as times have not been alike, true political sagacity manifests itself in distinguishing that complaint which only characterizes the general infirmity of human nature, from those which are symptoms of the particular distemperature of our own air and season.[30]

As an historian of culture, Dawson tried to provide this discernment. He insisted that: "The problem that faces us today is, therefore, not so much the result of an intellectual revolt against the traditional Christian morality; it is due to the inherent contradictions of an abnormal state of culture."[31] The late George Grant said that technology is the "ontology of the age".[32] Although Dawson himself never used these exact words, "ontology of the age", they convey his fully considered judgment of the state of modern society.

The modern religions of progress, including liberalism, were religiously heterodox expressions of the older Christian and humanistic culture. Liberalism could be understood in older, more familiar categories. Technologism, however, is something brand new. In the face of the technological society, the culture-forming mission of Christianity will have to begin from scratch —but begin at a much lower level than did the missionaries of the Dark Ages, who brought the vestiges of high Roman culture to the barbarian peoples of northern Europe. The *Venerable Bede* and *St. Boniface*, however, did not have to teach those Celtic and Gothic peoples the rudiments of culture itself. It was a dark age, but it was dark, Dawson said, "with the honest night of barbarism".[33] The terrifying thing about modern barbarism is that it is not only more culturally primitive than barbarians of old, but it is immeasurably more powerful, prosperous and ruthless.[34]

Born in the waning Victorian liberal culture, Dawson lived to see its demise. By the end of his career, Dawson seemed to understand that the new culture is something for which there is no history, for it has no precedent. Perhaps the verdict is still out on the Islamic states, who are attempting to preserve a traditional religious culture even while embracing the necessities of modern technology. But everywhere else, traditional cultures have folded under the technological order. I cannot think of a single success story of a society preserving its humanistic culture against technology. Even the Catholic Church, which has longer experience than any institution in dealing with bad governments, with human frailty, with heretics and ideologues of every stripe, nevertheless seems deeply perplexed at how to deal with a people who are convinced that their everyday well-being depends upon the technological order—on what the Encyclical *Veritatis splendor* calls the "all-intrusive culture".[35]

St. Boniface instructed the pagans not to worship a tree, for which he was martyred. But what is the proper address to the technological society? To give up the contraceptives but keep the microwaves? To use machines in moderation? The difficulty in even formulating the issue accurately indicates the perplexing nature of the problem. Abstractly considered, most technologies are not in themselves designed for morally wicked ends; the distinction between proper and improper use is always relevant. But we are not speaking abstractly. Rather, we have investigated the problem of an ensemble of technologies with their corresponding cultural habits. Whereas the moralist will examine human choices one by one, focusing upon the particular act, the cultural historian is interested in cultural habits and institutions; for these trace out the actual and imaginative bounds of men and women as social beings. It is in this latter respect that the problem of modern technology is something more than the moral problem of individual choices. As any parent who has tried to discipline the television-watching habits of his children can attest, the moral effort of picking and choosing when and where to "plug in" does not adequately represent the full nature of the problem. George Grant has correctly pointed out that we cannot understand the novelty of our technological society until we appreciate the extent to which it is a "package deal".[36]

At least for me, it indicates that Dawson was on the right track when he called our attention to the dominion of technology and why it has changed the nature of the game. As a cultural historian, Dawson understood that the core of a culture is found once we locate the thing that the culture would never relinquish or even imagine itself relinquishing. I submit that in our case it is not individual liberty, or sex, and certainly not religion. It is not even the machine. Rather, it is the machine insofar as it promises an activity superior to the human act.

# NOTES

[1] *America and the Secularization of Modern Culture* (Houston: University of St. Thomas, 1960), p. 12.

[2] Ibid., p. 21.

[3] Ibid., pp. 18–19.

[4] Ibid., p. 25.

[5] *Syllabus of Errors* (1854), no. 69.

[6] *On Liberty* (Indianapolis: Hackett Pub. Co., 1978), pp. 61–62.

[7] Ibid., p. 67.

[8] Ibid., p. 69.

[9] *The Theory of Moral Sentiments*, ed. D.D. Raphael and A.L. Macfie (Oxford, 1979), vol. 6.

[10] *Enquiries into Religion and Culture* (New York: Sheed & Ward, 1933), p. 62.

[11] *Religion and the Rise of Western Culture* (New York: Doubleday, 1958), p. 21.

[12] It is obvious that there is a profound difference between the old dualism of the Christian way of life and unregenerate human nature, on the one hand, and the new dualism between the revolutionary ideas of liberalism . . . , but there is a certain relation between the two, so that it is possible to maintain that the whole revolutionary tradition is a post-Christian phenomenon which transposes a pre-existent psychological pattern to a different sociological tradition. *Understanding Europe* (New York: Sheed & Ward, 1952), p. 28.

[13] *The Dynamics of World History* (LaSalle, Ill.: Sherwood Sugden, 1978), p. 355.

[14] *The Judgement of the Nations* (New York: Sheed & Ward, 1942), pp. 31–32.

[15] *America and the Secularization of Modern Culture*, p. 20.

[16] *The Judgement of the Nations*, p. 105.

[17] *Progress and Religion* (Peru, Ill.: Sherwood Sugden & Co., 1992), p. 207.

[18] *America and the Secularization of Modern Culture*, p. 17.

[19] *Progress and Religion*, p. 206.

[20] *The Judgement of the Nations*, pp. 31–32.

[21] *Progress and Religion*, p. 97.

[22] *The Judgement of the Nations*, p. 113.

[23] *America and the Secularization of Modern Culture*, p. 10.

[24] That is to say, techne is a substitute for praxis.

[25] Cited in Michael Adas, *Machines as the Measure of Men* (Ithaca, N.Y.: Cornell University Press, 1989), p. 226.

[26] Liberal culture sought to avoid the danger of complete secularization by insisting on the preservation of a margin of individual freedom, which was immune from State control and to which, in theory at least, economic life was subordinated. And within the zone of individual freedom, religious freedom was the ultimate stronghold which defended the human personality. But the progress of mechanization and the social organization which it entails has steadily reduced this margin of freedom, until today in the totalitarian states, and only to a slightly less degree in the democratic ones, social control extends to the whole life and consciousness. And since this control is exercised in a utilitarian spirit for political, economic and military ends, the complete secularization of culture seems inevitable. *The Judgement of the Nations*, p. 107.

[27] *The Judgement of the Nations*, p. 106.

[28] "The Patriarchal Family in History", *The Dynamics of World History*, p. 165.

[29] Ibid., p. 159.

[30] *Thoughts on the Present Discontents* (1770).

[31] "The Patriarchal Family in History", *The Dynamics of World History*, pp. 163–64.

[32] *Technology and Justice* (Notre Dame: University of Notre Dame Press, 1986), p. 32.

[33] *Christianity and the New Age* (Manchester, N.H.: Sophia Institute Press, 1985), p. 3.

[34] *The Judgement of the Nations*, p. 10.

[35] Pope John Paul II, Encyclical Letter *Veritatis splendor* (August 6, 1993), no. 88.

[36] *Technology and Justice*, p. 32.

GLENN W. OLSEN

# CULTURAL DYNAMICS:
# SECULARIZATION AND SACRALIZATION

We commonly speak of the profound secularization taking place in our times. Taking the long view, it seems that the race early on, wherever found, was God-connected and lived within a sacral order. Now such a condition of life is found in only the most isolated pockets outside, as the expression goes, the mainstream. This mainstream in the most obvious sense has been European, for if tracing secularization is our interest, it has been the peoples of Europe who have achieved the most spectacular secularization of life. They have, as Max Weber said, disenchanted the world.[1] We all know this has been by the most tortuous of routes, but there is just enough truth in Auguste Comte's Europe-based notion that mankind has passed through three ages, of theology, of metaphysics and of science, for us to see that it is especially European developments of the last millennium that have recast the once-sacred face of the earth. It is not that some such process has not been going on in all cultures we know anything about, nor that there is not a great variation among the non-European cultures in their experience and degree of sacralization. It is that the view of life we associate with the European Enlightenment has by now penetrated vast areas of the planet, so that in the most explicitly religious cultures which still remain, to have received a European form of education is likely to have become a member of a worldwide fraternity of the secularized, deracinated and perhaps sceptical about the very category of the sacred.

Yet, almost in the same breath with which we speak of

our times as novel in the degree and pervasiveness of secularization achieved, we also commonly describe the great mass-
movements of the age, Nazism or Marxism, for instance, as
new forms of religion, new forms of ultimate concern.[2] The
biblical parable seems to have taken on startling immediacy:
secular man, having driven out the unclean spirit of religion
from life, is faced with seven new demons, that is, transmuted
forms of faith which make all that was most distasteful in the
old religions seem almost benign in comparison with these new
products of possibly the most dreadful of human centuries yet.
The confidence of the secularized that one can have a public
morality in the absence of religion increasingly falls in doubt.
Questions multiply. Is it possible that what the Europeans have
been doing for these last centuries is committing cultural sui-
cide? Is it possible that, as Christopher Dawson held, religion is
so much at the center of what defines any culture that removing
or marginalizing it is tantamount to destroying the coherence
and continuity of the culture itself? Finally, does the appearance of the irrationality of the mass movements suggest that if
we break the intimate tie between Christianity and rationality,
forged against not a little opposition and expressed classically
in the Augustinian "I believe in order to understand" and
worked out in the harmonization of faith and reason by the
scholastics of the Middle Ages, what results is the worst form
of attachment to the sacred, which is ultimate commitment
untempered by reason?

Clearly secularization is not the one-way street taken un-
critically it may seem to be. To live at the end of this most
frightening of centuries is perhaps to have gained enough perspective on what has been going on to suspect that at least in
historical times sacralization and secularization have marched
hand in hand. They have gone on simultaneously, one area of
life sacralizing, one secularizing. For someone of my age, as it
was for Christopher Dawson, it is almost instinctive, in view
of the loss of influence of Christianity in the West, to think
in terms of an increasing tempo of secularization, in which

the very community of discourse on which any view of the world depends has been deeply eroded. Yet the new-old religions of the twentieth century, embracing a wide range of experience from the revival of the various fundamentalisms to the continuing vigor of nationalism, stand as warnings that we must examine this instinctive inclination to see secularization as a one-way street. In the present essay, I want to argue three things: (1) that the historical record provides ample evidence of a simultaneous dynamic of secularization and sacralization at work across the cultures; (2) that neither process is to be approved or disapproved unqualifiedly; and (3) that a proper Christian understanding of this cultural dynamic may be raised on Philippians 2:5–16, verses which are in part, appropriately enough, the Second Reading of the Twenty-sixth Sunday in Ordinary Time. The Jerusalem version translates these verses as follows:

> In your minds you must be the same as Christ Jesus:
> His state was divine,
> yet he did not cling
> to his equality with God
> but emptied himself
> to assume the condition of a slave,
> and became as men are;
> and being as all men are,
> he was humbler yet,
> even to accepting death,
> death on a cross.
> But God raised him high
> and gave him the name
> which is above all other names
> so that *all beings*
> in the heavens, on earth and in the underworld,
> *should bend the knee* at the name of Jesus
> and that every tongue should acclaim
> Jesus Christ as Lord,
> to the glory of God the Father.

... Do all that has to be done without complaining or arguing
and then you will be innocent and genuine, *perfect children of God
among a deceitful and underhand brood*, and you will shine in the
world like bright stars because you are offering it the word of
life.

I would in making my third argument like to show the significance of the biblical idea of being in but not of the world,
elaborated I believe in the passage just quoted, for a theory of
how sacralization and secularization are to be judged.

A definition of terms is in order. If I can stay close to the
Latin origins of our two terms, sacralization and secularization,
the former, as derived from the adjective *sacer*, means "conse-
crated to a divinity, holy, *or* sacred" or, as derived from the
verb *sacro*, means "to declare or set apart as sacred". I think
some precision will result if our use of the term sacralization
stays close to *sacro*, for I want to stress that sacralization is
a kind of declaration or setting apart of something as sacred.
Obviously at certain stages of culture the question of degree
of conscious intent arises, but in defining sacralization I want
to take as archetypical the practice of ritual purity. That is,
and we may use the development of Judaism as an example,
whatever the ultimate origins of a given purificatory rite, at
some point this rite was consciously understood as a means of
dedicating some practice or area of life to God or the gods.
Such an idea, as in the practice of kosher, may be extended to
all of life. This becomes a declaration that all is placed under
the will of God or that one intends to live a life of purity
before God. Usually the implication is that outside the area of
purity is an area of impurity, at least an area less directly God-
connected. Herein lies one possible ambiguity in the contrast
between sacred and secular. On the one hand, one meaning of
secularization will be to separate or remove something from
a previous connection to the sacred. However, it is possible
that some activity, perhaps wood-whittling or fastening one's
clothes, never was understood as particularly connected to the
sacred, that is, always was secular. In this case, secularity refers,

not to the end product of desacralization, but merely to some area of life which was never particularly God-connected or was always susceptible to being understood in some measure in its own right, whatever its relation to God. The Greek discovery of medicine is an example.

If with Mircea Eliade we understand the sacred as a declaration of what in life is most real, we have an adequate root idea of sacralization. Sacralization is a way of professing God-connectedness, that our lives are to be arranged around the highest reality, God. Obviously certain phenomena usually taken to be religious, specifically Buddhism in its most ancient form (the later development of the Buddha as avatar and savior introduced a theistic element not present in early Buddhism), present a problem for such a definition. For instance, whereas in most Western religion there was a development in the understanding of man and the cosmos in which a cluster of notions centered around the idea of individuality and personhood increasingly came to the fore, applicable as much to God as to man, a kind of movement from *animism* to the Fatherhood of God, nothing quite parallels this in ancient Buddhism. That is, there is nothing in Buddhism very similar to the Mediterranean developments, sometimes called the discovery of the individual, in which humans came to unify their souls so that an *ego* was seen at the center of a person, and an already personal God was, with Christianity, described as being composed of persons.[3] Buddhism by contrast retained its ties to notions of reincarnation and *karma* while elaborating the philosophical idea of *sunyata*, emptiness, or transcendence of all oppositions. Although there is some parallel between the Christian idea of *kenosis*, that the self must be emptied and die before it can be born again, and Buddhist *sunyata*, the dynamics of the two religions are very different. At the end for the Christian lies *theosis*, divinization, life more abundant; at the end for the traditional Buddhist lies emptying achieved, passionlessness, release, tranquility, transcendence. Of course this too is a kind of claim about what is "most real", and, as much as Christianity, Buddhism, even in its early form, has at least some of the links of a "great chain of being". Nirvana (not a term that bulks large in earliest Buddhism) is a permanent reality. Nevertheless, the problems in thinking about Buddhism, even in its more monistic and theistic forms, in terms of sacred and secular are formidable. From one point of view, the animist side suggests the presence of sacred categories everywhere. From another point of view, the world itself seems so transient and unreal as to lack any secular coherence or independence. But it is not clear that this means that indeed for Buddhism only the category of the sacred exists, for the idea of "most real" is unclear and indeterminate.

In general some form of "the great chain of being" is necessary for the polar distinction between sacred as "most real" and secular as "less ultimate" to appear, but in Buddhism in its first form what we have of such a chain does not lead "up" to a most real. There is rather a kind of movement of separation from a transient world, perceived as not very real, to stillness. If Christopher Dawson correctly characterized this religion, its "world-fleeing" aspects are so thorough-going that they may be said only to come to rest in the Beyond itself.[4] Where the Trinity, the living God, stands in Christianity, *sunyata* or emptiness stands in Buddhism.[5] Opinions in fact differ on how Buddhism in its many forms is to be understood, but if the final word is emptiness or nonbeing, then Buddhism is at once the ultimate secularization, declaring that there is no "most real" around which to order life, but also the ultimate sacralization, declaring that nothing in this world is substantial and that somehow we must leave it. In any case, to stay with my definition, if Buddhism originally was "godless", it had the form but not fully the substance of a sacral position. For the rest, any form of ultimate commitment, whether to money, race or nation, which is not clearly God-directed also may be spoken of as having the form but not wholly the substance of the sacral, and thence Marxism can be seen as asking religious commitment for the pursuit of a worldly or secular goal rather than for pursuit of the reign of God. In the degree to which any movement is characterized by an articulate pursuit of some highest good, it is sacral in form if not in substance, and we can expect such movements until the end of time.

Secularization, by contrast, is a word derived from the Latin *sæculum*, which, from the root meanings of "race" or "generation", was used by ancient Christian writers to designate the biblical *æon*, the "world" or "worldliness". Although in Christian tradition as it developed into the Middle Ages being "secular", that is, a layman, often implied inferiority and contrast to being "religious", that is, a monk, this distinction also had the more neutral sense of simply contrasting two modes of life, one lived in the world and the other in a monastery shut off from the world. Thus for the Carolingians around 800, *monachica vita* was a life directly oriented to God and in that sense not of the world, whereas the layman who lived out his life in the world, normally in the married state, was a *vir sæcularis*.[6]

It is good to keep in mind here the whole Pauline notion of man as "caught between the æons", between what is disappearing or losing reality and what is appearing or gaining reality, between the old and new man. This is directly relevant to the idea of being in but not of the world. In Matthean terms, "the reign of God is among you", that is, that which is most real has entered time and now dwells in the *sæculum*, this age. The very notion of being secular, that is, "of this world", implies contrast with not being of this world, that is, with sacrality. Indeed, one can argue that the idea of secularity depends on that of sacrality, that their relation is not bipolar, if that implies equal status at the opposite ends of a spectrum. Even if we could get beyond the historical evidence to show that some activities have definitively never had much of a sacral connection, these could only have been perceived as secular if the sacred was already in place as that against which the secular was contrasted. The secular is a category which appears in the midst of the sacred and only is conceivable with the sacred as a backdrop. The one depends on the other. A sacral society has a definite form and can stand by itself. Secularity, like the Aristotelian idea of matter or the Neoplatonic idea of evil, is not something that exists in or can stand by itself but merely marks the limits of intelligibility, the disappearance of any definite form, order or hierarchy of being.

Christian man, to return to our definition of terms, from the first was seen as caught between the æons. To repeat, the problem of how to relate sacred and secular in the Christian West was an exegesis of the command to "be in but not of the world". To speak of a *sæculum* did not imply that "the age" was of no value but that it did have about it an impermanency that made man a *viator*, or wayfarer, in it because he was, finally, made for something greater. This is a sense of the secular which I want to recover here. Secularity, whatever its other meanings, can designate a proper use of this world.

Some perspective here is necessary. In a number of profound works, Josef Pieper worked out philosophically an idea also found in many of Christopher Dawson's books, namely, that human life began in wonder and contemplation.[7] Pieper's attention was directed toward the Greek beginnings of Western thought, but writers as different as Lucien Lévy-Bruhl and Eric Voegelin have written of a universal "matrix": "Anywhere in the world, if one goes back far enough, one comes upon a worldview that can be described quite adequately as mythological—that is, one comes upon a world that is permeated with sacred, divine forces."[8] One of the reasons for Christopher Dawson's deep appreciation of the Eastern religions was that they had with considerable success looked beyond the passing to that which in some sense endures. Pieper stressed that Mediterranean philosophy itself emerged from the more primordial religious act of contemplation, of receptivity before being. Indeed philosophy was a kind of second-level reflection on man's primordial orientation, a striving for coherence and clarity about what is implied in man's being oriented in awe to the world. If Peter Berger is right that the "mythological matrix" is characterized by wholeness, that is, by fluid or permeable boundaries between men, nature and the gods, we might speak of the birth of philosophy itself as a form of secularization, a subjecting of what was whole and undifferentiated to analysis and classification.

It is a commonplace that in comparison with our Faustian civilization the Mediterranean long lived under the sign of *teoria*, with its greatest thinkers praising *bios teoretikos*, a life lived in pursuit of knowledge for its own sake. Of course few were philosophers, even citizens, but leisure and the enjoyment of public beauty, the latter a reflection both of the beauty of nature and of man's capacity for "improving on nature", bulked large in life for generations. Societies which had about them the face of hardness, of strong class solidarity and unconcern for the unfortunate nevertheless also were marked with a strong sense of the beauty of this world, to be contemplated and complimented by taking advantage of glorious natural sites for construction of the works of human genius, whether temple, theater or city itself. Before ever there was a Christianity, the ancient world lived by grace.

One of the stunning achievements of the Golden Age of Greece was, in a still god-connected world, the way in which philosophy, that is, reason's study of our orientation to being, clarified the range of human capacity, or searched out the secular world. Homer had not been sure of whether the world had a history if one tracked back even three generations before Troy. Herodotus, by travelling to Egypt and studying the records of the priests, discovered at once how young a civilization his own was and how much longer the "time of man" had been than Homer supposed. That is, while not denying the place and influence of the gods in the world, Herodotus engaged in a great act of secularization, of seeing in his imagination that one's family line did not descend from the gods nearly as recently as Homer had supposed. Homer, in fact, was a lying poet, who had sketched a world so god-connected as not to appreciate how long man's career had been. Thus with Herodotus the "time of the gods" receded and the "time of man" extended. To pursue the argument outlined above, we may see this as a secularization proper to man, proper because discovering what lies within human capacity without severing the primordial orientation to God or being which also defines mankind.

The second of the surviving Greek historians, Thucydides, did not merely follow Herodotus' path but saw the importance of a parallel secularization achieved by Hippocrates, Thucydides' good friend. Hippocrates thought it insufficient merely in the traditional manner to attribute sickness to the will of the gods. It might very well be true that such was the case, but this was at a level of causation outside, except by prayer, man's powers. For Hippocrates the interesting question was what man could control. Here Hippocrates moved more clearly from contemplative to power categories, from accepting the world as it is to in some way modifying it. By patient observation he discovered, or made more precise the knowledge of, the fact that human diseases have observable courses. By chronicling day by day the changes in his patients, he discovered a this-worldly knowledge of disease, the cure of which could be sought not in prayer, or not only in prayer, but in treatment. Hippocrates had discovered the distinction between primary and secondary causation, between what is the work of the gods and thus inscrutable—although one could always try the oracles—and what is knowable and a possible subject of human control. We might say that the category of primary causation, of explaining effects by reference to God as cause, retained a kind of sacrality, while the category of secondary causation, explaining effects by reference to observable interworldly chains of causation, articulated a sphere or powers proper to man in the *sæculum*. Thucydides filled his history with historical analysis in the mode of the physicians, showing for instance civil war as a public disease with its own stages of development. But it was in the "Melian Debate" of his great history that he used Hippocrates' distinction with a vengeance. Whenever the hapless Melians refused to face questions of power and of facts about the world anyone could discover and threw their hopes in the laps of the gods, retreating back into a sacral order, the Athenians brought them back to secular reality, brazenly noting that even the gods understand and obey the rules of power.

Aristotle, the Philosopher, as the Middle Ages were to call him, has a special importance in the history of the dynamic relation between secularization and sacralization. Thus far, because the sacral backdrop is in place when the historical record begins, I have been detailing instances of secularization, but my first argument is that secularization and sacralization normally occur simultaneously. It would not be difficult to show the persistence of sacred categories, or instances of a kind of re-sacralization of life, in ancient times. Both Greeks and Romans remained fascinated with questions of the relation of the human and the divine, for instance, of the "ontological" boundaries between the two. Still in the fifth century, Sophocles ended his Theban trilogy with Oedipus, the blind man who now could see, not dying, but surefootedly in his blindness walking off-stage to be with the immortals. And still in the fifth century the centuries-old project of unifying the human person continued apace. In comparison to Homer's characters, whose emotions were as often as not not their own but of doubtful origin, sensations which arose in the breast coming from only the gods knew where, the characters in fifth-century drama are more self-possessed, if not more responsible. Although there are wild moments, Plato's *psyche* is relatively unified, even classified.

Aristotle stands apart from all his contemporaries in many ways, but I think his power of clearing the fog from historical analysis is underreported. This power marks an important stage of secularization, a secularization, to follow my second argument, which clearly allowed humans to have a surer grip on the world. Eliade has remarked that almost all the religions and therefore all the cultures of the world begin with a "once upon a time", with a best time when people were close to the gods and often lived in an egalitarian state of life without private property, law or the state. This Eden or Age of Saturn was then lost, but the recovery of what it possessed was an implicit goal of subsequent life. This continuing attempt to re-cover the original matrix of life was one of the prime instances, running throughout the cultures of the world, of resacraliza-tion, of recovery of an earlier and better stage of life. But, in my opinion, this was a kind of not facing facts, a bad form of resacralization, if you please. A secular reality, in this case the fact that, at any period of which we have any record, we find that humans are unequal by nature, as Plato and Aristotle observed, was denied. This form of resacralization, of trying to recover an allegedly earlier and purer form of life, is found, not simply in the Marxist hope for the withering away of the State and the recovery of common property, but in age-old political projects, Virgil's hope for the recovery of the Age of Gold with Caesar Augustus, or the ever-present hope for *renovatio imperii*. We commonly find some such form of sacral wishfulness in many of the ancient authors, and I have argued elsewhere that it is the single most common way of approaching politics until the present.[9]

So far as I can see, Aristotle completely escaped such a point of view. For him, since there was no historical record of a best age of man now lost, there was no reason to speak of such. Not for him Hesiod's ages of half-gods-half-men or ages of gi-ants or men with life spans ten times that now experienced. If one stayed to the historical record, men seem to have been always pretty much what they are now. One finds in history no Edens, no original condition of life without society, law and authority. That is, one sees that man is by nature a politi-cal animal and that Greeks were merely the first to understand that private property, law and the State are not after-thoughts or remedies for the loss of some supposed first egalitarianism but things which exist in the degree that a given people have discovered the full range of man's this-worldly capacities. They may not have always existed, because man's potentialities are only discovered over the course of history, but they always will exist when the full implications of man's being made for political life are understood. There is no indication that Aristotle consciously saw his own way of approaching politics as a counter to the myths of beginnings which surrounded him: he merely avoided falling into the traps laid by them and, in so doing, displaced the gods from one more area of human life or revealed man in nature more clearly.

It hardly needs remarking that Aristotle did not desacralize the world in general. He merely continued the exploration of what is properly human. The fact that he proved the existence of God is not particularly important here in showing that, even if he agreed with Plato/Socrates that the things of God are far above us and dark, his world was God-centered. Much more important is his retention of the then already ancient idea that the contemplative life is so high that when we engage in it we broach the limits of our humanity and pass over to divinity. That is, just as we are of our nature oriented to the political life, we are oriented toward God. Likely Aristotle did not understand this God as coalesced, so to speak, around personhood: this indeed made man's passing over to divinity easier, for, as the Stoics were to see, what opens God, nature and man to each other is their common rationality, either their being rational or their embodiment of that which is intelligible.

The Jews, even disallowed by their God for a long time from having kings, had taken an arguably more tortuous and less satisfactory route to discovering the limits of human capacity. Still, as they came to see the significance of the difference between an eternal and a created world, between a "making" and a creator God, they achieved one of the central secularizations in the history of the world, the drawing of a clear line between Creator and creature. This purged nature of its divine mediations in a degree uncommon in the Mediterranean, or for that matter the rest of the world. Indeed, the perpetual temptation of the Jews to lapse into polytheism indicates the continuing appeal of return to an earlier, more fluid, cosmos in which God is not so clearly distinguished from man.[10]

The drawing of a clear boundary between God and man did not set up an unbridgeable gulf, for the Jews also affirmed that man was created in God's image. In a way different from Aristotle's, they insisted that there is a divinely oriented center to man. Although most Jews spoke with the language of the heart, at least some learned Jews, likely under the influence of Greeks, came to understand this God-connecting center to lie in the mind. In either case, though different, the languages of the two cultures could be translated into one another, so that Jew and Greek could recognize similar preoccupations in one another. While most people, Jew or Greek, lived in a rather undifferentiated divine cosmos, which left them open both to stories about earlier and more God-connected states of life and to a natural order occupied at every turn by nymphs, satyrs and vaguer pneumatic presences, an intellectual consensus was forming that man at his center was oriented to both the world and to God. In a sense this gave a sacred axis to life, centered on God and the soul, not present in the more diffuse sense of the sacred found among the less secularized.

Among pagan thinkers, the Neo-platonists especially were to work out this insight that in the highest reaches of his soul man is oriented toward God. The Christians, heirs to Jew and Greek, seized on the idea that man is made in the image of God to develop it in several directions. Words designating the center of man, where it was perceived that man had a center, had long varied. The philosophers perhaps tended to mind- or *nous*-centered words, but it was not simply Christians who, following many Jews, spoke of the heart as at the center of human beings.[11] In any case, whatever the language used, and commonly it was the language of the heart but of a heart which was at once desiring and contemplative, Church Fathers like Origen brought the various traditions together in a vision in which humanity retained a sacred center.

Space does not allow for portrayal of the many secularizations and sacralizations to the present. By definition the story
is not progressive or in any easy sense developmental. In some
ways, for instance, the Germanic peoples brought with them
into Europe a less secularized and differentiated society than
the Romans had developed. Thus in the investiture struggle
of the eleventh century, with its attempt to distinguish once
more between the things of God and of man, a kind of secularization of Germanic theocratic notions took place. From the
Church's side, long-standing Germanic royal sacral claims were
rejected. The result was a less fluid and whole world, one in
which kingship had been largely demoted from its sacral status
to be identified as dealing with *temporalia*. We find somewhat
similar processes at work across the globe. Thus the Japanese
scholar Yamamoto Shin (1913–80) suggested that there are
three types of secularization. We can not pursue this here, but
the conflict between *regnum* and *sacerdotium* in eleventh-century
Europe clearly exemplifies Yamamoto's first type, in which
conflict between the religious and military powers causes secularization.[12]

Christopher Dawson argued in book after book that one
of the things that lent the Western Middle Ages its particular
dynamic was the fact that from the beginning it lacked wholeness, that is, an integrated and stable sacral cosmos. Learning,
the drive for peace and the new religion or idea of the sacred
were largely in the hands of monks and clergymen commonly
carrying Mediterranean ideals with them. Political and military power and old sacral ideas most commonly were in the
hands of the rulers of the Germanic peoples. Much of the medieval story revolves around the struggles, compromises and
assimilations made between these two forces and the ways in
which the sacral conceptions of each modified the other. Modern Neoplatonists like Eric Voegelin have lamented the breakdown of the sacral cosmos which we find in the investiture
struggle, or later in Thomas Aquinas' distinction between faith
and reason. Presumably, and with much justification, granted

the last five hundred years of European history, the fear is an autonomous, Cartesian reason which forgets its mooring in man's original orientation to God.[13] But it seems wrong to me to criticize clear advances such as Aquinas' achievement of a principled distinction between faith and reason simply because it undoes a previously less differentiated world and opens a host of possible abuses, including improper notions of autonomy.

Some medieval thinkers themselves had a sense of the dangers here but did not on this account give up their attempt to understand this world. Thus, possibly with the tendency in mind of certain writers such as Bernardus Silvestris and Alanus de Insulis to create a "free-zone" for man in relation to God, more autonomy than the Christian tradition suggested man had, late twelfth- and early thirteenth-century legal scholars, facing the parallel question of the autonomy of nature, came to gloss the word *natura*: "*id est, Deus.*"[14] This was no pantheistic affirmation but a counterweight to classical freight borne by the word *natura*, specifically its personification in a Dame or Mother Nature who could be seen as autonomous and not subject to God, even as God's replacement. To guard against such ideas, these scholars, upon invoking "nature", hastened to add either that *natura* was a personification standing in for God or that, although the realm of nature might have its own integrity, it still fell under God's rule, was God's agent and expression. The secular realm remained God-connected. The belief long had been that God had written two books, the Bible and Nature, and that he was revealed in both. Study of nature could as much lead to him as away from him: "*per creaturas ad creatorem*", a great twelfth-century theme, was still affirmed by Newton.

More than Voegelin's, Dawson's eyes were fixed on the emergence of modern practices of freedom, which he saw precisely to be one of the fruits of the struggle between Church and State.[15] Dawson's instinctive sense that there was health in the struggles to define jurisdictions seems to me more pene-

trating that Voegelin's lament over a lost world. In some ways
Dawson's view is vindicated in a recent, stunning book by
Eamon Duffy, which, in showing the vitality of late medieval
Catholicism in England until the rupture caused by the Reformation, studies late medieval people's experience of the holy
in detail. Duffy shows the interweaving of sacral categories,
such as the liturgical calendar, and secular time.[16]

Dawson always saw the interplay between sacred and secular
as in principle enriching. Culture itself, after all, for him was
embodied religion, a temporal, material and passing expression
of that which surpasses all such categories. If I may express it
this way, in religion-formed culture the ever-changing may be
seen also under an eternal perspective. The sacred and secular
come together so that the secular, while of this world, is not
without orientation to the reign of God which is only glimpsed
in this world. This is the point of my invocation of Philippians
2:5–16 to make my third argument, that both secularization
and sacralization are to be judged from the perspective of a
stance in but not of the world. These verses say that Christ
having humbled himself to enter our *sæculum* was raised on
high so that all beings should bend the knee to his name and
acclaim him Lord. Christians are to be God's perfect children
among a deceitful brood, shining in the world and offering it
the word of life. Note, these verses do not say that every being will bend the knee, that is, that ever in history the Gospel
will unqualifiedly triumph. They merely say that every knee
should bow, that is, that the goal to which Christians always
labor is the communication of the word so that people freely
bend the knee. Further, there is no suggestion that in history
the deceitful brood will disappear. The image communicated
is that of the Christian trying to be perfect, thus radiating into
the world the glory of God, the needed word of life. In the
language of the present essay, we should assume the persistence
of sacralizing and secularizing tendencies to the end of time,
some of which are good, some bad. The Christian's goal, the
Church's goal, in all situations is to be a shining into time of

that which both entered time and is above time. As Hans Urs von Balthasar put it, the Church is to interpret the "signs of the age", be yeast of the world, and mediator of salvation to it.[17] I perhaps should add that fear today that the Western world is too secular should not blind us to the opposite possibility, a too sacral world, dominated by primary causation or a kind of theological imperialism in which humans cannot express all the capacities native to them.

From Judaism Christianity inherited a powerful idea used in the exploration of the *sæculum*. This was the idea that humans are to be *dominators*, lords of the earth. In some sense, as the Church Fathers put it, humans were cocreators with God, made to continue the creative work of God. In the Middle Ages this idea was developed almost in disregard of the doctrine of original sin by the aforementioned Bernardus Silvestris in his creation allegory, *De Mundi Universitate*. In this work man is not simply the culmination of the creation but in turn the perfector of the newly made world: the world cannot attain its fullness without man's effort.[18] The larger point is that the Church cannot in principle be separated from the world, although this is a perpetual temptation and sometimes for centuries has in some degree been a dire necessity. That is, called to domination or stewardship, the Christian sees the inadequacy for a fully human life of either contemplation by itself or the quest for power by itself. As historical and bodied but also spiritual creatures, we are ordered both toward sacrality and toward secularity. I suppose this is the point of the insistence of both Augustine and Aquinas that contemplation is not an end in itself for the Christian but is to be oriented in charity to our brethren in society. Neither, *pace* Sir Francis Bacon, is the quest for power over nature our end. Much ancient and medieval theory of the beautiful saw art, a work of beauty specific to man, as an improvement on nature, and this seems to me to be the key. According to the Christian understanding, as stewards human beings are placed in nature to exercise their talents over it, but only in ways that truly improve life in society, that is, improve nature by intelligence.

Above I suggested that one basic meaning of secularization was the removing of the connection between some activity or area of human life and religion or the sacred. Thus recently, in regard to the commemoration of the twenty-fifth anniversary of *Humanæ vitæ*, Bishop James T. McHugh noted that "one of the results of secularization is the removal of marriage and family life and sexuality from their religious roots and relationships."[19] Here Bishop McHugh conceived of secularization not just as the severing of specific activities from religion but as a cumulative or large-scale process which had more or less simultaneously severed large areas of life from their earlier religious sources. Marriage, we might say, previously understood as a sacrament which imitated the unseverable nuptial relation and fidelity between Christ and the Church, had become a contractual relationship severable at will. The family, previously viewed as a domestic church imitating the life of the Trinity, had become merely a convenient arrangement for ordering one's life, so malleable that it could be established by "spouses" of the same sex. Sexuality, previously understood as at least analogous to the *eros* that draws all to God, had become merely a form of entertainment or gratification. That is, the cumulative effect of individual secularizations had been to create a new kind of world from which more and more the framing of life by religion disappeared, so that secularization seemed almost a state of being. To use Marxian terms, sufficient quantitative changes had created a basic qualitative shift. The separate secularizations reinforced one another and came to compose a secular world.

From what has already been said, it is clear this is not the whole story, for the argument has been that secularization and sacralization take place continuously. Thus what we must say is that the previous historical associations between specific activities and religion have, at least in the West, largely been severed by our day, only to be replaced by new religious expressions, running the gamut from Marxism to jogging as a way of achieving a "natural high". The large question is what our prospects for the future are. Is the logic of liberalism and large-scale secularization such that all future resacralization will be piecemeal and isolated? If so, can there be any meaningful *Recovery of the Sacred*, to use the title of a splendid book, in one area, as the liturgy, without the recovery of supporting ideas in society at large?[20]

My view is that forms of liberalism and secularism similar to that of John Rawls, specifically by rejecting all that falls under the old heading of the common good, are to be seen as forms of anarchism, that is, of a radical individualism centered on rights which in principle prescinds from the idea of a shared public life. Their logic is forever to lead to society's disintegration. Whether this in fact will occur I do not know. There is a powerful reason arguing, rather, for the ultimate failure of the liberal project, and that is mankind's ineradicable religious nature. But the reassertion of religion, especially an improperly secularized religion, that is, a religion without long traditions of faith being harmonized with reason, is not a necessarily pleasant prospect. On this scenario, we may be faced with periodic pendulum swings between the anti-authoritarian solvent of liberalism and the fascist attempt of wholeness. Wholeness, or what in theology has been called integrism, does not seem to me in the cards: never really was in the cards. Change is too central a category to being in history, and man too much the sinner this side of the grave, for the wholeness of primitivist aspiration ever to come to pass.

I think our best secular hope is that there is some parallel between the history of civilization and the history of philosophy. That is, as Étienne Gilson attempted to show in *The Unity of Philosophical Experience*, given enough time there is a kind of corrective at work in this world in which really dreadful roads wrongly taken reveal themselves. The history of the whole civilization is infinitely more complicated than the history of philosophy, but it is arguable that correction really does occur.

It is not just that Romanticism, if itself unbalanced, was a true corrective to the Enlightenment. The fall of the Berlin wall, whatever the messy aftermath, did spell the end of a form of life which had become intolerable. Powerful voices like that of Andrew Louth have for some time been showing how we may disengage ourselves from seriously mistaken premises common now in the culture for centuries but above all to be associated with the superficiality of the Enlightenment.[21]

The Enlightenment, while taking important steps forward in secularization, for instance, in the discovery of man's critical skills, also, especially, in its Deist conception of God, that is, its secularization and domestication of God into banal categories, seriously misunderstood the ways God is present in the world. From such misunderstanding, in which effectively the Creator disappeared and man became the author of himself, it was not a long step to the modern sense of alienation, for little remained of a sacral cosmos in which humans could find their place. Mark R. Schwehn has written a powerful book both analyzing this last development and arguing against the desirability of the form the intellectual life took in *The Education of Henry Adams*. Schwehn holds that for the life of the mind to prosper a kind of desecularization must take place in which the community on which disciplined educational conversation rests is reconceived as spiritual in nature, more oriented toward contemplation than power.[22]

P. D. James has recently written a novel which imaginatively captures correctives arguably already at work. One of her themes is, in the words of a reviewer, "the uselessness of liberal theology in a time of profound crisis".[23] Liberal theology, with its enlightenment or secular meliorism, is simply inadequate when one contemplates the dangers and disasters of the twentieth century: "In such a world people will hold to a fully supernatural faith—in which hope is quite specifically a *theological virtue*—or they will abandon hope altogether." I doubt if it is quite as simple as this, but James has seized the central point, seen clearly two generations ago by Romano Guardini,

that in the postmodern world, characterized for those with eyes
to see by danger, the theological virtues—the God-connecting
virtues, if you please—will come to the fore.[24] The Christian's
duty will be seen, not to be to make the world whole, but to
allow an image of God to radiate into it, so that the age will
have its witness.

Christopher Dawson could not believe that the anti-authoritarian destructiveness of liberalism and secularism was the last
stage of our history. I would suggest that the path he laid out
more than a half-century ago in *Progress and Religion* is as fresh as
when first presented. Assuredly Western culture is even more
fragmented than in Dawson's day, and we rightly wonder if
there will ever be much common to the civilization again.
Yet, as an act of the imagination, Dawson opens to us the
kind of world for which on the most favorable reading we
may hope and work. Assuming that because we are religious
animals the religious impulse will always assert itself in one
way or another, Dawson closed his great book with the following sentences:[25]

> The vital and creative power behind every culture is a spiritual
> one. In proportion as the spiritual element recovers its natural
> position at the centre of our culture, it will necessarily become
> the mainspring of our whole social activity. This does not, how-
> ever, mean that the material and spiritual aspects of life must
> become fused in a single political order which would have all
> the power and rigidity of a theocratic state. Since a culture is es-
> sentially a spiritual community, it transcends the economic and
> political orders. It finds its appropriate organ not in a state, but
> in a Church, that is to say a society which is the embodiment
> of a purely spiritual tradition and which rests, not on material
> power, but on the free adhesion of the individual mind. It has
> been the peculiar achievement of Western Christianity in the
> past to realize such an ideal in an organized spiritual society,
> which could co-exist with the national political units without
> either absorbing or being absorbed by them. The return to this
> tradition would once more make it possible to reconcile the ex-
> istence of national independence and political freedom, which

are an essential part of European life, with the wider unity of our civilization, and with that higher process of spiritual integration which is the true goal of human progress.

# NOTES

[1] Weber's 1918 address, "Wissenschaft als Beruf", with its appropriation (secularization) of religious language to describe the academic life, is brilliantly criticized in Mark R. Schwehn, *Exiles from Eden: Religion and the Academic Vocation in America* (New York: Oxford University Press, 1993). Talal Asad, *Genealogies of Religion: Discipline and Reasons of Power in Christianity and Islam* (Baltimore, Md.: Johns Hopkins University Press, 1993), issued too recently to be used in the present study, challenges much in traditional (liberal) presentation of the story of secularization.

[2] J. Budziszewski, "The Illusion of Moral Neutrality", *First Things* no. 35 (August/September 1993), pp. 32–37 at 36, prefers a trichotomy to the dichotomy "religious" and "secular": "An acknowledged religion like Christianity or Buddhism posits an ultimate concern and admits it. An unacknowledged religion like Leninism posits an ultimate concern but denies that so doing is religious. And an incomplete religion like Millianism [a reference to John Stuart Mill] has not finished ranking its concerns."

[3] I have sketched the outlines of this development in "St. Augustine and the Problem of the Medieval Discovery of the Individual", *Word and Spirit: A Monastic Review* 9 (1987), pp. 129–56.

[4] *Christianity and the New Age* (London, 1931; reprinted with new Introduction by John J. Mulloy, Manchester, N.H.: Sophia Institute Press, 1985), as at pp. 23, 56.

[5] Cf. Roger Corless and Paul F. Knitter, eds., *Buddhist Emptiness and Christian Trinity: Essays and Explorations* (New York: Paulist Press, 1990), and Donald W. Mitchell, *Spirituality and Emptiness: The Dynamics of Spiritual Life in Buddhism and Christianity* (New York: Paulist Press, 1991), which compares Buddhist emptiness (of the Kyoto School) and Christian *kenosis* (self-emptying).

[6] Jean Chélini, *L'Aube du moyen âge, Naissance de la chrétienté occidentale: La Vie religieuse des laïe dans l'Europe carolingienne* (750–900) (Paris: Picard, 1991), pp. 35–37.

[7] See especially *Leisure, the Basis of Culture* (New York: Pantheon Books, 1952). Cf. Jean-Luc Nancy, *The Birth to Presence*, trans. Brian Holmes, et al. (Stanford, Calif.: Stanford University Press, 1993).

[8] Peter L. Berger, "God in a World of Gods", *First Things* no. 35 (August/September 1993): pp. 25–31 at 29, for the quotation and what follows.

[9] Most recently in "John Rawls and the Flight from Authority: The Quest for Equality as an Exercise in Primitivism", forthcoming in *Interpretation: A Journal of Political Philosophy*.

[10] Berger, p. 29 (above n. 8). Berger lists various other quests for wholeness to the present.

[11] I have traced some of the history of the language of heart and mind in "Twelfth-Century Humanism Reconsidered: The Case of St. Bernard", *Studi Medievali*, 3a serie, 31 (1990), pp. 27–53.

[12] See the analysis of Masaki Miyake, "The Concept of Time as a Problem of the Theory of Civilizations and History", *The Bulletin of the Institute of Social Sciences*, Meiji University, vol. 15, no. 3 (1992), pp. 1–18 at 5–6. The second type is "renaissance", in which an earlier period, perceived as less sacral than the present, is consciously sought out, and the third type is "conflict between orthodoxy and heterodoxy". Yamamoto gives European and Eastern examples of the three types, each a kind of emancipation from religion.

[13] Andrew Louth, *Discerning the Mystery: An Essay on the Nature of Theology* (New York: Oxford University Press, 1983), gives an overview and has penetrating things to say about Cartesianism and its heirs.

[14] C. Stephen Jaeger, *Medieval Humanism in Gottfried von Strassburg's Tristan und Isolde* (Heidelberg: Winter, 1977), pp. 7–16, has highly interesting things to say about Bernardus, Alanus and the "free-zone": see also the following, with n. 18 below. Gaines Post, *Studies in Medieval Legal Thought: Public Law and the State, 1100–1322* (Princeton: Princeton University Press, 1964), pp. 504–5, 522, 537ff., 551–52, treats "natura, id est, Deus".

[15] I have discussed Dawson's interest in freedom in "The Maturity of Christian Culture: Some Reflections on the Views of Christopher Dawson", in *The Dynamic Character of Christian Culture: Essays on Dawsonian Themes*, ed. Peter J. Cataldo (Lanham, Md.: University Press of America et al., 1984), pp. 97–125 as at pp. 102, 104–5.

[16] *The Stripping of the Altars: Traditional Religion in England c. 1400–c. 1580* (New Haven, Conn.: Yale University Press, 1992), with the useful review by Maurice Keen, "That Old Time Religion", *The New York Review of Books* 40:15 (September 23, 1993), pp. 50-51.

[17] *Razing the Bastions: On the Church in This Age*, trans. Brian McNeil, foreword by Christoph Schönborn (San Francisco: Communio Books, Ignatius Press, 1993).

[18] See, for example, *The Cosmographia of Bernardus Silvestris*, trans. Winthrop Wetherbee (New York and London: Columbia University Press, 1973), p. 113, with Jaeger, pp. 7–9, 39, and above n. 14.

[19] Quoted in "'Humanæ Vitæ' Teachings Valid Despite Dissent", *Intermountain Catholic* 55:26 (August 6, 1993).

[20] My "The City in Christian Thought", *Thought* 66 (1991): pp. 259–78, is a meditation on one array of issues treated by James Hitchcock, *The Recovery of the Sacred* (New York: Seabury Press, 1974). See also Bernard Lewis, *Islam and the West* (New York: Oxford University Press, 1993), which, while frequently misdescribing Christianity, deals with the question of the persistence of non-

secular categories in the modern world; and the review by Shaul Bakhash, "Intimate Enemies", *The New York Review of Books*, 40:16 (October 7, 1993), pp. 43–45.

[21] See above, n. 13.

[22] See above, n. 1.

[23] Alan Jacobs, review in *First Things* no. 35 (August/September, 1993): pp. 48–50 at 49, for this and the following quotation.

[24] See my "Christian Faith in a Neo-Pagan Society", in the book of the same title, ed. Paul L. Williams (Scranton, Penn. 1981), pp. 16–34.

[25] (Peru, Ill.: Sherwood Sugden & Co., 1992), pp. 249–50.